DEADLY DUDES

Dr Peter Bonadie and Dr Elsworth Neale

Copyright Page

© 2025 DR PETER BONDIE AND DR ELSWORTH NEALE

All rights reserved.

No part of this publication may be reproduced, distributed, or transmitted in any form or by any means, including photocopying, recording, or other electronic or mechanical methods, without the prior written permission of the publisher, except in the case of brief quotations embodied in critical reviews and certain other noncommercial uses permitted by copyright law.

For permission requests, please contact: (Apostlebonadie@gmail.com)

This is a work of faith-based nonfiction. The author affirms that the content is based on personal experience and Scripture, but it is not intended as professional medical or psychological advice. Readers are encouraged to consult qualified professionals for personal health and wellness matters.

Cover design by Mr. Lester Ifill

Printed in The United States of America

ISBN 979-8-9997718-0-3

First Edition

Dedication

This book is dedicated to every woman who has silently suffered beside a man who was supposed to protect her heart but instead pierced it. It is for the countless wives who lost pieces of themselves trying to hold their marriages together while enduring manipulation, neglect, or emotional torment. It is for the brave women who walked away—not because they stopped loving, but because they finally started loving themselves enough to leave what was destroying them.

To those still caught in the storm of confusion, pain, and prayer—may this book be your mirror, revealing the truth; your map, guiding you to freedom; and your mantle, covering you with the strength to reclaim your voice. You are not crazy. You are not alone. And you are certainly not to blame.

God sees you. God knows your tears. And God is still the Healer of broken hearts and the Restorer of shattered hope. May every page breathe clarity, courage, and healing into your soul.

Acknowledgement

Writing this book has been both a burden and a balm. It was born out of years of listening to the silent cries of women whose pain was often minimized, dismissed, or misunderstood. I am deeply grateful to every woman who found the courage to share her story, even through trembling lips or tear-filled eyes. Your vulnerability has given voice to countless others, and your strength has helped shape the pages of this work.

I want to thank the pastoral counselors, marriage mentors, and mental health professionals who provided wisdom and insight during the development of this book. Your expertise has ensured that these truths are not only biblically grounded but also psychologically sound. To my research assistants and editors—your diligence and attention to detail brought clarity and structure to complex topics, and I am indebted to your excellence.

To my closest circle—thank you for keeping me grounded, praying for me when the emotional weight became heavy, and reminding me of the importance of this assignment. You know who you are, and I honor you.

Above all, I acknowledge the Spirit of God, the Wonderful Counselor, who grieved with me as I wrote and gave me language for the anguish that so many endure in silence. May this book be a tool for healing, truth, and transformation.

Table of Contents

DEDICATION iii
ACKNOWLEDGEMENT iv
FOREWORD 1
PREFACE 3
INTRODUCTION 5
   When the Man Becomes the Storm *5*
CHAPTER 1 7
   The Narcissist, All About Him *7*
CHAPTER 2 13
   The Absent Man, Physically Present, Emotionally Absent *13*
CHAPTER 3 18
   The Controller, Master of Domination *18*
CHAPTER 4 23
   The Critic, nothing is Ever GOOD Enough *23*
CHAPTER 5 29
   The Cheater, The Unfaithful Husband *29*
CHAPTER 6 35
   The Addict, Substance and Sexual Bondage *35*
CHAPTER 7 41
   The Angry Man, Explosive and Unsafe *41*
CHAPTER 8 47
   The Passive Man, Present But Powerless *47*
Chapter 9: 53
   The Deceiver, Living a Lie *53*
CHAPTER 10 58
   The Silent Abuser, When the Wounds Are Invisible *58*

CHAPTER 11 64
The Mama's Boy, Married to His Mother 64

CHAPTER 12 69
The Hypocrite, Double Life, Double Standard 69

CHAPTER 13 74
The Dream Killer, Crushing Her Potential 74

CHAPTER 14 79
The Dangerous Dudes in the Bible 79

CHAPTER 15 86
When Women Break 86

CHAPTER 16 92
The Journey to Healing, Rebuilding After the Ruin 92

CHAPTER 17 98
The Religious Manipulator, Misusing God to Control Her 98

CHAPTER 18 104
The Criminal Husband, When Silence Becomes Complicity 104

CHAPTER 19 115
Keys to Choosing a Good Mate, Wisdom Before the Wedding .. 115

CONCLUSION 129
From Miserable to Mighty — The Exit from Bondage 129

APPENDICES 132
Appendix A 132
Appendix B 134
Appendix c 135
Appendix D 136
Appendix E 137
Appendix F 138

FOREWORD

Marriage is one of the most sacred institutions ordained by God, designed to reflect His covenantal love and mutual submission between Christ and the Church (Ephesians 5:25–33). Yet, for many women, marriage has become a source of sorrow rather than a sanctuary—a battlefield instead of a blessing. While much has been written about submission, roles, and the beauty of marital unity, too little has been said about the toxic behaviors of men who misuse their position, distort Scripture, and devastate the very women they vowed to cherish.

Dangerous Dudes: Men Who Make Marriage Miserable is not an angry tirade against men, nor is it a bitter commentary on broken homes. Rather, it is a bold exposé, written with the fierce compassion of a shepherd and the surgical precision of a truth-teller. Dr. Peter Bonadie dares to articulate what many women feel but are afraid to say: that some men—despite being charming, accomplished, or even religious—can be emotionally unsafe, spiritually manipulative, and psychologically destructive.

This book names what others avoid. It challenges the silence that has enabled dysfunction and spiritualized abuse in the name of leadership. With biblical authority and psychological insight, Dr. Bonadie dissects the traits of narcissists, controllers, deceivers, dream-killers, mama's boys, and hypocrites—holding them up to the light of God's Word and exposing the damage they cause. He does not generalize or bash men; he identifies specific patterns that cause women to suffocate in relationships that should have brought them life.

What makes this book profoundly healing is its commitment to restoration. It not only describes the problem—it equips readers to discern, avoid, and heal from it. For single women, it provides discernment. For married women in pain, it offers clarity and courage. For pastors, counselors, and mentors, it serves as a handbook for intervention and guidance.

As you read, be prepared to weep, to see your story, and to finally have language for your pain. But also be prepared to rise. There is hope in truth, and truth has power. This book will not only open your eyes—it will empower your spirit.

If you have ever been silenced, confused, blamed, or broken in the name of love, then this book was written for you. And if you are a man with the courage to read it, you may just find the mirror your soul needs and the map your masculinity requires.

Preface

I never set out to write a book that would make some men uncomfortable—but I knew I had to write one that would set some women free.

Dangerous Dudes was born not just from theological study or pastoral counseling, but from real-life anguish poured out in quiet rooms, whispered phone calls, and desperate prayers from women who loved deeply but suffered silently. These women weren't rebellious. They weren't ungodly. They weren't trying to escape God's design for marriage. They were simply asking: Why is this so painful when it's supposed to be sacred?

Over the years, I've encountered patterns—repeat offenders in character, behavior, and spiritual distortion—embodied by men who claim to love but don't know how to lead, protect, or nurture. Some were ignorant. Others were indifferent. A few were malicious. But all left behind a trail of broken spirits, weary hearts, and confused wives who kept asking God, *Is it me?*

This book is my answer: No, daughter, it's not you. It's the dysfunction you've been trying to normalize.

In these pages, you'll read about different types of destructive male behavior—ranging from the narcissist to the hypocrite, the dream-killer to the religious manipulator. You'll see biblical examples, real-life scenarios, and practical insights for recognizing these dangerous traits early. You'll also find redemptive wisdom—because God is not only a Revealer of error, but He is also a Restorer of hope.

Dangerous Dudes is not an indictment of all men. It's a clarion call to accountability, to healing, and to righteous relationships. My prayer is that it will give voice to the voiceless, strength to the weary, and clarity to those confused in the fog of marital misery. I also pray it will challenge good men to rise higher and become safe spaces for the women they love.

Whether you are single, married, divorced, or in the process of discerning your next step, this book is for you. I encourage you to read it slowly, pray through its truths, and allow the Holy Spirit to illuminate areas in need of healing, correction, or courage.

May the light of God expose every darkness hiding behind charm, charisma, or spiritual clichés. And may you, dear reader, walk boldly into the freedom, wisdom, and love you were always meant to receive.

With a shepherd's heart and a warrior's fire!

INTRODUCTION

When the Man Becomes the Storm

Marriage was never meant to feel like survival. It was designed to be a covenant of safety, love, partnership, and purpose. But what happens when the man who stood at the altar becomes the source of your pain? What do you do when the very hands that held you now control you? When the voice that once comforted you now criticizes you? When the one who promised to lead you is the one who breaks you?

This book was born from a burden to speak into a silent epidemic—relationships where women are slowly dying inside because the men they married are emotionally unsafe, spiritually immature, or outright manipulative. These men may not wear the label of "abuser." They may quote Scripture, serve in ministry, and appear noble to the outside world. But behind closed doors, they inflict wounds that sermons never mention, and their wives carry invisible scars that go unnoticed in Sunday services.

Dangerous Dudes is not a book about male-bashing. It is a truth-telling, lie-breaking, darkness-exposing, dignity-restoring manual. It is a mirror for those who dare to look and a map for those who want to escape. It identifies twelve distinct male archetypes—types of men who make marriage miserable not necessarily through fists, but through manipulation, neglect, control, passivity, or spiritual distortion.

These are not caricatures or exaggerations. They are patterns—repeated in counseling sessions, whispered in confessionals, written in journal entries, and felt in the hollow stares of women who gave their all and got nothing in return. These men include the Narcissist, the Controller, the Manipulator, the Passive Pretender, the Hypocrite, and the Dream Killer. Some are emotionally absent. Others are religious tyrants. But all of them are destroyers of intimacy, trust, and feminine identity.

As you read, you'll be invited into stories, biblical insights, psychological truths, and practical wisdom. You will be challenged to reflect, to discern, and, perhaps most importantly, to heal. Some of you will see the red flags you ignored. Others will understand for the first time why you've been miserable, even while married. Still others will find language for wounds that had no name.

This book is also a warning to those who are not yet married. Marriage does not fix character flaws—it magnifies them. Who you choose to marry will shape your destiny, your peace, your emotional stability, and even your relationship with God. Choosing poorly can cost you decades. But choosing wisely, through discernment and divine guidance, can be one of the greatest blessings of your life.

To the men who are willing to read this with humility—this is your mirror. If you see yourself in these pages, don't run. Repent. God is not done with you. But He cannot heal what you deny. He cannot deliver what you defend. And He cannot bless what you keep hidden in the dark.

This is a dangerous book because it dares to speak the truth. But it is also a hopeful book—because where truth reigns, healing can begin.

To every woman reading this who has ever asked, *Is it me?*, this book answers: *No, it's not you. But now it's time to deal with what it really is*. Welcome to the truth.

CHAPTER 1

The Narcissist, All About Him

Marriage is meant to be a reflection of Christ's love for the Church—sacrificial, tender, faithful, and deeply considerate. In **Ephesians 5:25**, Scripture commands, *"Husbands, love your wives, just as Christ loved the church and gave himself for it."* This divine standard sets the tone for a husband's responsibility—not just to be present, but to be emotionally engaged, sacrificial in affection, and intentional in honor. But what happens when the man at the altar is consumed not with his bride, but with himself? When his love is transactional, his praise is selective, and his empathy is absent? That man is what we call the narcissist—a dangerous dude cloaked in charm but void of the selflessness that makes love thrive.

Narcissism is not just a personality quirk or egoism taken too far; it is a deep-seated behavioral pattern that erodes relationships, especially in marriage. The term finds its roots in Greek mythology—Narcissus, the young man who fell in love with his own reflection, unable to look away even as he withered. In modern psychological language, narcissism involves an inflated sense of self-importance, a craving for admiration, and a striking lack of empathy for others. In marriage, this becomes deadly. The narcissistic husband does not enter into union with the intent to build a life together, but to construct a kingdom where he is both ruler and god, expecting perpetual validation and unquestioned obedience.

From the beginning, God said in **Genesis 2:18**, *"It is not good that the man should be alone; I will make him a helper suitable for him."* The helpmate was not made to be a shadow, an echo, or an emotional slave. She was designed as a co-laborer, a partner suitable for him, equal in worth and dignity. Yet in the hands of a narcissist, this divine arrangement is desecrated. The wife becomes a tool to prop up his fragile ego, a mirror that must only reflect adoration, and a vessel robbed of her voice.

The narcissistic husband rarely starts as a tyrant. He is often alluring in courtship—charming, confident, articulate, and even spiritual. His charisma masquerades as leadership; his intensity is mistaken for passion. **Proverbs 14:12** warns, *"There is a way which seems right to a man, but its end is the way of death."* What seemed like the right choice in dating becomes a nightmare in matrimony. Over time, the mask slips. Affection turns to arrogance. The listening ear is replaced with deflection. Every disagreement is an attack on his superiority, and every challenge to his decisions is viewed as rebellion.

Narcissists are masters of manipulation. In a marital context, they rewrite narratives to always emerge as the victim or hero, never the villain. When a wife confronts him about emotional neglect or inconsistency, he pivots the conversation. Suddenly, she is "too sensitive," "never satisfied," or "always complaining." This gaslighting distorts her reality, making her question her sanity and blame herself for the emotional coldness she feels. This is not love; this is warfare. And the narcissist arms himself not with fists but with confusion, shame, and psychological erosion.

The Bible is not silent about such behavior. In **2 Timothy 3:2–5**, Paul describes the moral decay of the last days: *"For men shall be lovers of their own selves, covetous, boasters, proud, blasphemers, disobedient to parents...without natural affection...lovers of pleasures more than lovers of God; having a form of godliness, but denying the power thereof."* This portrait of spiritual emptiness mirrors the heart of a narcissist. He may wear the costume of righteousness—serve in church, quote Scripture, lead prayers—but his heart is devoid of divine compassion. The form is present; the power is not.

Many women in narcissistic marriages suffer in silence because the abuse is not always physical. It's mental, emotional, and spiritual. The wounds are invisible but deep. She walks on eggshells, not because he has raised his hand, but because he constantly undermines her worth. He withholds affection as punishment, delivers praise as manipulation, and uses Scripture to justify domination. He might quote **Ephesians 5:22**—*"Wives, submit yourselves to your own husbands"*—while conveniently omitting verse 25, which requires him to die to self as Christ did for the Church. That selective theology is not spirituality; it is spiritual abuse.

In **Matthew 23,** Jesus rebukes the Pharisees for their hypocrisy, saying, *"For they bind heavy burdens, grievous to bear, and lay them on men's shoulders; but they themselves will not move them with one of their fingers"* **(v. 4)**. The narcissistic husband behaves in a similar fashion—placing expectations on his wife that he refuses to live by himself. He demands forgiveness without apology, loyalty without investment, and respect without reciprocity. He believes he is owed honor simply for existing, not for the character he demonstrates.

One of the most painful aspects of being married to a narcissist is the loneliness. The wife may be surrounded by people yet feel utterly alone. Her cries are met with cold logic. Her tears are minimized as "overreaction." Her dreams are dismissed as distractions from his agenda. **Song of Solomon 2:15** warns us to *"catch the foxes, the little foxes, that spoil the vines."* Narcissism is one of those little foxes. It creeps in silently, undetected during dating, and slowly chokes the emotional vine of the marriage. What could have been a thriving vineyard becomes a barren wasteland.

It is also important to note that not all narcissists are bold and brash. Some are covert. They play the victim, manipulate with guilt, or present themselves as martyrs. They give just enough affection to keep the relationship afloat but never enough for it to flourish. The wife is left feeling confused—never quite able to articulate what's wrong, but knowing something is broken. **Proverbs 12:18** says, *"There is one who speaks like the piercings of a sword, but the tongue of the wise brings healing."* The narcissist's words may not be loud, but they are sharp. Over time, the wife bleeds internally—emotionally and spiritually.

The impact on children must also be acknowledged. When a man is consumed with himself, he becomes emotionally unavailable not only to his wife but also to his children. He teaches sons to devalue women and daughters to accept emotional neglect as normal. **Exodus 20:5** speaks of iniquity visiting *"the third and fourth generation."* Narcissism, when unchecked, becomes a generational curse. If the cycle is not broken, the damage multiplies across decades.

But there is hope—even for the narcissist. Though deeply entrenched, narcissism is not an unpardonable sin. Transformation begins with truth. **James 3:14–16** says, *"But if you have bitter envying and strife in your hearts, do not glory and lie against the truth… For where envying and strife are, there is confusion and every evil work."* The narcissistic man must stop lying to himself. He must confront the mirror—not to admire his reflection, but to confess his need for God. True healing begins when he lays down his pride and picks up a cross.

Luke 9:23 says, *"If any man will come after me, let him deny himself, and take up his cross daily, and follow me."* This verse is the antidote to narcissism. The call to follow Christ is a call to die—to ego, to entitlement, to self-exaltation. A man cannot serve his ego and his wife at the same time. He must choose. And until he chooses to follow Christ with humility, he will continue to devour the garden of his marriage with the locusts of selfishness.

In practical terms, repentance for the narcissistic husband means seeking counsel, submitting to spiritual authority, and humbling himself in conversation with his wife. It means validating her pain, apologizing without defensiveness, and becoming a student of her soul. **Colossians 3:19** declares, *"Husbands, love your wives, and be not bitter against them."* Bitterness toward a wife often stems from insecurity in the man. When a husband refuses to deal with his inner wounds, he projects those fractures onto the woman God gave him to love.

The Church must also do better. Too often, narcissistic men are shielded in religious spaces because they tithe well, preach powerfully, or maintain a good reputation. But Jesus warned in **Matthew 7:16**, *"You shall know them by their fruits."* A man may have the gifts of the Spirit but still lack the fruit of the Spirit. Galatians 5:22–23 tells us that love, gentleness, and self-control are the marks of Spirit-filled living. If a man is constantly harsh, prideful, and self-serving, then his fruit reveals his true root.

Wives in such marriages need clarity and courage. Clarity to know they are not crazy, and courage to draw boundaries. They must stop enabling dysfunction in the name of loyalty. Love does not mean silence. Love does not mean suffering without confrontation. **Proverbs 27:5** says, *"Open rebuke is better than secret love."* Speaking up is not rebellion—it is righteousness. God is not honored by a peace that comes from pretending.

To the man reading this chapter who sees himself reflected in its mirror—this is your invitation to change. God is not looking to condemn you, but to refine you. **Isaiah 57:15** says, *"I dwell in the high and holy place, with him also who is of a contrite and humble spirit."* You do not have to continue being the dangerous dude. You can become the healed husband. But you must first admit: it's not all about you.

To the woman reading this chapter who has wept silently, walked on eggshells, and prayed for breakthrough—know this: God sees. He is not blind to your tears or deaf to your prayers. **Psalm 34:18** says, *"The*

Lord is near to them that are of a broken heart." God is near, and He is not impressed by the image your husband projects. He knows the truth, and He will sustain you, vindicate you, and—should you need to walk away—guide you.

Marriage was never meant to be the graveyard of joy. While no spouse is perfect, there is a vast difference between imperfection and intentional destruction. The narcissistic man makes the marriage about his crown, not her comfort. But there is a better way. It begins with Christ, who, though He was God, *"made himself of no reputation, and took upon him the form of a servant"* **(Philippians 2:7).** Let every man who wants to lead in love start by serving, sacrificing, and seeing his wife not as a reflection of himself, but as a reflection of God's grace.

Chapter 2

The Absent Man, Physically Present, Emotionally Absent

One of the most devastating forms of abandonment in marriage is not physical desertion, but emotional withdrawal. The absent man is not the husband who has left the home, but the one who has vacated the marriage emotionally, mentally, and spiritually while still sharing the same roof. He is there—but not really. He sleeps in the same bed but is unreachable. He shares meals but not conversation. He finances the house but not the heart. This absence is not seen in his body, but in his silence. And it leaves a wound no one else may notice, but his wife lives with daily.

In **Genesis 2:24**, God said, *"Therefore shall a man leave his father and his mother, and shall cleave unto his wife: and they shall be one flesh."* The cleaving here is not merely sexual or residential; it is emotional and spiritual. To cleave means to cling with intention—to be bound together in purpose, in presence, and in participation. The emotionally absent man violates this divine principle by disconnecting his soul from the union, reducing his role to a provider or supervisor while his wife starves for affection, attention, and affirmation.

Emotional absence is subtle but suffocating. It is the slow erosion of intimacy, often undetected in its early stages. The wife may excuse his silence at first: "He's just tired," "He has a lot on his mind," or "He's not good with words." But eventually, the excuses no longer comfort her soul. What began as a trickle becomes a drought. Conversations become mechanical. The only questions he asks are logistical: "Did you pay the bill?" "Did the kids finish their homework?" Never, "How are you really feeling?" or "What's been weighing on your heart lately?" The woman begins to wither in a relationship that looks alive but is dying from the inside out.

Scripture emphasizes the power and necessity of presence. In **Matthew 1:23**, Jesus is called *"Emmanuel,"* which means *"God with us."* The very nature of divine love is presence. God didn't love us from a distance—He came near. He entered our pain, walked our roads, and engaged our hearts. A husband who seeks to love his wife as Christ loves the church must learn the power of emotional presence. Being physically available is not enough. God did not send a letter; He sent Himself. Love shows up with its heart, not just its body.

The emotionally absent man often doesn't see himself as destructive because he equates faithfulness with staying. "I'm still here, aren't I?" he might say defensively. But proximity is not the same as intimacy. You can sit next to someone on a long flight and never know their name. In the same way, many wives share space with men who haven't touched their souls in years. They co-parent, co-exist, and co-manage, but they do not co-love. This emotional vacancy fosters resentment, loneliness, and, eventually, bitterness.

Proverbs 18:22 says, *"He who finds a wife finds a good thing, and obtains favor from the Lord."* But how does a man honor the gift he has found if he refuses to emotionally unpack his own heart? The emotionally absent man is often guarded, wounded, or emotionally illiterate. He may have never seen emotional connection modeled growing up. Perhaps his father was stoic, or his culture praised men who were silent and detached. Yet the call of God upon the husband is not to replicate dysfunction but to reflect Christ. Christ did not emotionally ghost His bride—He engaged her. He wept with her, celebrated with her, listened to her, and ultimately died for her.

Emotional absenteeism in marriage leads to many subtle yet severe consequences. The wife feels invisible. She begins to second-guess her worth. Her longing for intimacy, which is God-given, goes unmet. **Proverbs 13:12** teaches, *"Hope deferred makes the heart sick, but when the desire comes, it is a tree of life."* When a woman's desire for connection is continually denied, her heart begins to grow sick—not with sin, but with sorrow. She may start to shut down, mirroring his detachment to protect her own soul from further injury.

This detachment often spills into the spiritual realm. The emotionally absent husband is rarely the spiritual priest of the home. He may attend church, but he does not lead in prayer. He may provide financially, but he does not guide the household in worship. He relinquishes his role as spiritual covering, forcing his wife to carry both the emotional and spiritual burden alone. In Ezekiel 34:4, God rebukes the shepherds of Israel, saying, "The diseased you have not strengthened, nor have you healed what was sick… but with force and cruelty you have ruled them." While this rebuke was aimed at leaders, its principle applies to the home. A husband who neglects the emotional health of his wife rules not with gentleness, but with cruelty—whether he realizes it or not.

Emotional absence also opens doors for temptation. When a woman is consistently emotionally starved, she becomes vulnerable—not because she is unfaithful by nature, but because she is human. Her need for conversation, affection, and connection doesn't disappear; it simply looks for a place to breathe. Many affairs don't begin with lust but with loneliness. A kind voice, a listening ear, or a gentle word can become a lifeline for a woman drowning in emotional neglect. This is not a justification for infidelity but a warning: when a man withholds emotional intimacy, he plants seeds that the enemy is more than willing to water.

The emotionally absent man also often fails to validate his wife's emotions. He may see her as "too emotional" or "dramatic." He may shut down during arguments or avoid conflict altogether. This avoidance is not peace; it is passivity. **Ephesians 4:26** says, *"Be angry, and do not sin: do not let the sun go down on your wrath."* When issues are not addressed, resentment builds. And when a man refuses to engage emotionally, he leaves wounds to fester. He mistakes silence for resolution and disengagement for peacemaking.

In marriage, silence is not neutral—it is formative. Silence shapes how a woman sees herself. When she is ignored, she internalizes that as unworthiness. She may start to question her beauty, her intelligence, and even her spirituality. The enemy capitalizes on this silence, whispering lies that multiply in the void the husband refuses to fill. 1 Peter 3:7 instructs husbands to "dwell with them according to knowledge, giving honor to the wife, as to the weaker vessel." This knowledge is not intellectual; it is emotional. It means studying her heart, learning her fears, affirming her dreams, and showing up when she's fragile.

There is also a cost to the man himself. Emotional detachment in marriage is often a reflection of deeper wounds in the man's soul. He may be emotionally absent not because he doesn't care, but because he doesn't know how to care. He may be carrying unhealed trauma, shame, or confusion. But hiding behind detachment only perpetuates brokenness. Psalm 147:3 says, "He heals the broken in heart, and binds up their wounds." God is willing to heal the emotionally absent man—but healing requires exposure. It requires a willingness to confront the pain he buried long ago.

Restoration begins with small steps. Emotional presence doesn't mean being perfect, poetic, or always knowing what to say. It means being available, curious, and engaged. It means asking questions, listening without interrupting, sitting in silence without rushing to fix, and validating feelings without dismissing them. Emotional presence says, "I see you. I care. I'm here." These simple actions become sacred bridges between hearts that have drifted apart.

One of the most powerful examples of emotional presence in Scripture is seen in John 11. When Jesus saw Mary weeping over the death of her brother Lazarus, He did not rebuke her. He did not deliver a theological lecture. He wept with her. John 11:35 simply says, "Jesus wept." In that moment, divinity embraced vulnerability. That is what emotional presence looks like. It's not about having all the answers—it's about showing up in the pain.

The emotionally absent man must make a decision: to continue hiding or to return home—not just to the house, but to the heart of his wife. Hosea 2:14 says, "Therefore, behold, I will allure her, and bring her into the wilderness, and speak comfortably to her." God Himself is a model of emotional re-engagement. Even when His people strayed, He pursued them with tenderness, not detachment. A husband who desires to heal his marriage must follow this divine example—pursuing, listening, and restoring.

To the woman who has suffered in silence, you are not alone. God is not absent, even if your husband is. Psalm 34:17 reminds us, "The righteous cry, and the Lord hears, and delivers them out of all their troubles." Keep crying. Keep hoping. Your tears are not wasted. Your heart is seen.

To the man who recognizes himself in this chapter—there is no shame in beginning again. Ask God to teach you how to feel, how to engage, how to love deeply. And ask your wife for grace as you relearn what presence truly means.

A home without emotional connection is merely a shared space. But a marriage anchored in presence becomes a sanctuary. The emotionally absent man may not have left physically, but his return begins with a decision: to show up, to speak up, and to love not just in deed, but in heart.

CHAPTER 3

The Controller, Master of Domination

Among the most oppressive and spiritually damaging husbands is the controlling man—the master of domination. His presence is overbearing, his expectations suffocating, and his affection conditional. He rules the home with an iron hand, cloaked either in silent intimidation or loud verbal assertion. Unlike the narcissist who seeks admiration, the controller demands obedience. His world is one of compliance and submission, where disagreement is rebellion and autonomy is insubordination. This man weaponizes authority, often misinterpreting biblical headship as a license for tyranny. The controlling husband is not a leader in the biblical sense—he is a manipulator, an emotional hostage-taker, and a destroyer of joy.

Scripture speaks clearly against such misuse of authority. In **Matthew 20:25–26**, Jesus draws a distinction between worldly domination and godly leadership: *"You know that the princes of the Gentiles exercise dominion over them, and those who are great exercise authority over them. But it shall not be so among you."* Jesus did not call husbands to dominate their wives; He called them to serve them. The controlling man distorts this call and turns covenant into captivity. He lords over his wife as if she is his property, not his partner.

One of the chief characteristics of a controlling man is fear-driven manipulation. He operates under the illusion that if he does not control everything, he will lose everything. This fear translates into micromanagement—of her thoughts, her schedule, her friendships, her clothing, even her spirituality. He may disguise his domination as "protection" or "guidance," but at the root is deep insecurity. His soul is restless unless everything and everyone bows to his version of order. **Proverbs 29:25** says, *"The fear of man brings a snare: but whoever puts his trust in the Lord shall be safe."* The controlling man has not trusted God with his wife—so he tries to play God himself.

Often, such men are skilled at presenting themselves as righteous. They may be deacons, pastors, or faithful attendees in the pews. They quote **Ephesians 5:22** often: *"Wives, submit yourselves to your own husbands, as to the Lord."* But they misuse this verse as a whip, not as a call to mutual honor. What they forget—or choose to omit—is the preceding verse: *"Submitting yourselves one to another in the fear of God"* **(Ephesians 5:21),** and **verse 25**: *"Husbands, love your wives, just as Christ loved the church and gave himself for it."* The controlling man is selective with Scripture, using the Bible not as a mirror for his soul but as a tool to dominate hers.

In practice, the controller may forbid his wife from working, not out of conviction but insecurity. He may isolate her from friends and family, monitoring her communications and questioning her every move. He makes her feel guilty for having a life outside his orbit. This behavior is not headship—it is harassment. **Galatians 5:1** reminds us, *"Stand fast therefore in the liberty with which Christ has made us free, and do not be entangled again with the yoke of bondage."* A marriage rooted in domination is not freedom; it is a yoke.

Another tactic of the controller is verbal policing. He corrects her constantly, often in front of others. He dismisses her ideas, critiques her opinions, and subtly (or overtly) discredits her contributions. His goal is not conversation but control. He wins arguments not with truth but with force. The wife, over time, becomes silent—not because she agrees, but because she fears. Proverbs 15:1 says, "A soft answer turns away wrath: but grievous words stir up anger." But the controller does not use soft answers. His tone is always final, his words always louder.

This pattern produces a toxic atmosphere in the home. The wife becomes emotionally paralyzed, unable to express her true thoughts without fearing retaliation. She suppresses her opinions to keep the peace. She second-guesses her instincts. Her creativity withers. She becomes a version of herself that she no longer recognizes. Meanwhile, the husband feels vindicated. "She's quiet because she respects me," he may think. But what he sees as respect is actually resignation. Psalm 55:21 exposes this pattern: "The words of his mouth were smoother than butter, but war was in his heart: his words were softer than oil, yet were they drawn swords."

Some controlling men are not loud—they are emotionally cold. They withhold affection as punishment. They give the silent treatment to provoke fear or submission. Their control is not through forceful words but through withdrawal. This emotional manipulation makes the wife feel abandoned unless she complies. It is a psychological war—she is being trained like Pavlov's dog: obey and receive warmth; resist and receive coldness. This is not love—it is coercion.

Biblically, the model of true headship is Jesus Christ. How did Christ lead the Church? By dying for her. By washing her feet. By bearing her burdens. Philippians 2:6–7 says of Christ: "Who, being in the form of God, did not consider it robbery to be equal with God: but made himself of no reputation, and took upon himself the form of a servant." The controlling man makes himself of much reputation. He craves being right, being honored, and being feared. But the godly husband seeks to serve—not to subdue.

An often-overlooked aspect of the controlling husband is spiritual abuse. He dictates how his wife should pray, when she should fast, and which spiritual leaders she can listen to. He may use spiritual language to justify domination, saying things like, "God told me," as a way of ending all discussion. This is extremely dangerous. It robs the wife of her agency and spiritual discernment. 1 John 2:27 declares, "But the anointing which you have received from him abides in you… and you need not that any man teach you." A woman filled with the Spirit has access to divine wisdom. A husband's role is not to monopolize God's voice but to support his wife in hearing God for herself.

The story of Nabal and Abigail in 1 Samuel 25 is a vivid biblical example of a controlling man. Nabal was described as "churlish and evil in his doings" (v. 3). His arrogance and refusal to listen nearly brought destruction on his household. Abigail, his wife, had to intervene with humility and wisdom to avert a disaster. Later, God judged Nabal for his behavior. The lesson is clear: God sees the inner workings of households. He holds men accountable for how they treat their wives—not just in public, but in private.

Control kills intimacy. It builds walls instead of bridges. It suppresses rather than supports. The wife of a controller often feels more like a prisoner than a partner. Even her spiritual growth becomes stifled. Her prayer life becomes filled with groans and tears. She may feel isolated, even from God, because the image of her husband has distorted her view of divine love. But the Lord is near. Psalm 34:18 declares, "The Lord is near to them that are of a broken heart; and saves such as are of a contrite spirit."

The legacy of a controlling husband also extends to the children. Sons grow up believing that domination equals masculinity. Daughters grow up believing that love must always feel like fear. The generational ripple is devastating. Yet Malachi 4:6 offers hope: "And he shall turn the heart of the fathers to the children, and the heart of the children to their fathers." Transformation is possible—but it starts with humility.

To the controlling man, let this chapter serve as a mirror. Look closely. Do you demand more than you serve? Do you listen less than you speak? Do you use Scripture to silence your wife instead of sanctifying her? If so, the call is not to shame but to repentance. James 4:6 reminds us, "God resists the proud, but gives grace to the humble." True manhood is not domination—it is sacrificial leadership. It is washing her feet, not walking over her soul.

To the wife under such control—God sees. You are not invisible. You are not crazy. You are not rebellious for having a voice. You were made in the image of God, not to be crushed under human pride but to flourish in mutual honor. There is wisdom in boundaries, strength in truth, and healing in the presence of God. Seek counsel, seek safety, and do not bear this burden in silence.

And to the Church—let us not enable controllers in the name of headship. Let us teach men that love leads with listening, not lording. That strength is shown in tenderness. That authority is validated by humility. Christ did not crush His bride—He carried her. Let every husband go and do likewise.

CHAPTER 4

The Critic, nothing is Ever GOOD Enough

Marriage was designed to be a place of mutual affirmation, where love builds, grace restores, and words uplift. It is in the context of marriage that the power of speech becomes most sacred, most vulnerable, and most consequential. Yet, for many wives, the home is not a refuge of affirmation—it is a battlefield of criticism. They are married not to an encourager, but to a critic. To a man whose words bruise instead of bless. A man for whom nothing is ever good enough. Not the cooking. Not the house. Not the way she dresses, raises the children, or even worships. This man is a dangerous dude—not because he hits, but because he hammers her soul daily with condemnation.

Proverbs 18:21 says, *"Death and life are in the power of the tongue: and those who love it shall eat its fruit."* The critic wields this power recklessly, sowing words that drain his wife's confidence and sense of worth. His speech is not constructive feedback rooted in love—it is an endless stream of fault-finding, sarcasm, and blame. His tone is sharp. His praise is rare. His compliments are usually backhanded. Where there should be edification, there is erosion.

The critical husband often sees himself as merely "honest," "realistic," or "holding high standards." But his constant commentary does not produce excellence—it produces exhaustion. A wife who can never meet the standard begins to feel like a failure even when she's giving her best. **Ecclesiastes 4:9–10** reminds us, *"Two are better than one… For if they fall, one will lift up his fellow."* But the critic never lifts. He steps over his fallen wife with a sigh and a lecture.

What makes the critic so dangerous is that his abuse is often invisible. There are no bruises to show. The damage is internal—mental, emotional, and spiritual. He tears down her ideas, mocks her opinions, and rebukes her efforts. Over time, the woman begins to internalize his voice as her own. "Maybe I am stupid." "Maybe I am lazy." "Maybe I am just not good enough." His criticism becomes her inner dialogue. This is psychological bondage masquerading as marital normalcy.

The Bible clearly condemns this kind of speech. In **Colossians 3:19**, husbands are warned: *"Husbands, love your wives, and do not be bitter against them."* Bitterness, often unhealed in the critic's heart, is projected onto the wife. Perhaps he's disappointed with his own life. Maybe he's carrying unresolved pain from his past. But instead of dealing with it, he blames and belittles his wife. His criticisms aren't really about her—they are the outflow of his own woundedness. **Luke 6:45** declares, *"A good man out of the good treasure of his heart brings forth that which is good… for out of the abundance of the heart his mouth speaks."*

The critic also often masks his behavior under the guise of spiritual leadership. He may claim he is trying to "help her grow" or "lead her into excellence." But the fruit of his speech is not maturity—it is fear. **1 John 4:18** says, *"There is no fear in love; but perfect love casts out fear."* If a wife is afraid to speak, afraid to fail, or afraid to dream because of how her husband will react, then she is not living in love—she is living under tyranny.

Critics rarely affirm. If they do offer praise, it is usually followed by a "but." For example: "The meal was good, but the rice was undercooked." "You look nice, but why that lipstick?" "I appreciate your help, but you always forget something." This pattern of conditional affirmation keeps the wife in a perpetual state of anxiety. She is always reaching, always striving, always second-guessing. Her soul becomes a tightrope walker—trying to please a man whose applause never comes.

In contrast, the Word of God calls men to build with their words. **Ephesians 4:29** says, *"Let no corrupt communication proceed out of your mouth, but that which is good to the use of edifying."* The word "edify" means to build up, like constructing a house. The critic does the opposite—he tears down. A wife's confidence is a construction site he demolishes daily with verbal wrecking balls. He may not raise his voice, but his words still shatter.

Another destructive trait of the critic is comparison. He may compare his wife to other women—his mother, his ex, or even fictional women from TV and social media. "Why can't you be more organized like so-and-so?" "Look how she dresses—why don't you try that?" These comparisons crush her uniqueness. They communicate one message clearly: "You're not enough." Yet the Bible declares in **Proverbs 31:29**, *"Many daughters have done virtuously, but you excel them all."* Every woman has her own glory, her own beauty, and her own grace. A wise husband celebrates that—he doesn't critique her for not being someone else.

The critic also damages intimacy. Emotional connection cannot thrive in an environment of constant fault-finding. The wife withdraws—not because she's cold, but because she's tired of being wounded. Intimacy becomes mechanical or nonexistent. Her body shuts down because her heart is wounded. **Song of Solomon 4:7** expresses the spirit of godly affection: *"You are all fair, my love; there is no spot in you."* This is not denial of imperfection—it is celebration of covenant. A wife who feels cherished becomes more beautiful, more alive. But the wife of a critic loses her glow. Her laughter fades. Her sparkle disappears.

One of the lesser-acknowledged outcomes of being married to a critic is spiritual discouragement. A woman married to a critical man may start to feel that God is also disappointed in her. She begins to project his displeasure onto the Lord. Her prayer life suffers. Her worship is strained. She no longer feels worthy of God's love because her own husband treats her as if she's always falling short. This is a spiritual emergency. The critic, in essence, becomes a false prophet of shame, standing in the place where affirmation should dwell.

A powerful example in Scripture of the danger of critical speech is found in Job's friends. They visited Job not to comfort but to critique. They accused him of hidden sin, implied that his suffering was deserved, and offered endless commentary instead of empathy. **Job 16:2 says**, *"I have heard many such things: miserable comforters are you all."* The critic is a miserable comforter. He is present but unhelpful. He speaks, but his words wound.

Some critics are sarcastic, using humor as a mask. They mock their wives in public, tease them in ways that sting, or joke about their "failures" as a form of passive aggression. **Proverbs 26:18–19** warns, *"Like a madman who casts firebrands, arrows, and death, so is the man who deceives his neighbor and says, 'Was I not joking?'"* Jokes that wound are not funny—they are emotional arrows. And when a wife expresses that she is hurt, the critic often responds, "You're too sensitive." This response is not only dismissive—it's cruel.

Why do some men become critics? Many were raised by critical parents themselves. They may have grown up in homes where affection was rare and performance was everything. They were praised only when they excelled and shamed when they failed. Now, as husbands, they replicate what was done to them. This is not an excuse, but an explanation. **Exodus 20:5** warns of generational patterns: *"visiting the iniquity of the fathers upon the children."* Criticism can be inherited—but it can also be broken.

Healing begins with acknowledgment. The critical man must see his speech as a weapon—not a tool. **James 3:6** warns, *"And the tongue is a fire, a world of iniquity... it defiles the whole body, and sets on fire the course of nature."* If his wife is emotionally distant, constantly anxious, or spiritually dry, he must ask: what have my words burned down in her?

Repentance includes more than an apology. It includes retraining the tongue. **Proverbs 15:4** says, *"A wholesome tongue is a tree of life: but perverseness therein is a breach in the spirit."* The critic has breached his wife's spirit. Now he must speak words that bring life. This doesn't mean flattery or fake compliments. It means affirming her efforts, thanking her for her sacrifices, and noticing her strengths. It means asking for feedback about his own behavior. A wise man not only speaks but listens. **James 1:19** instructs us, *"Let every man be swift to hear, slow to speak, slow to wrath."*

To the wife living under the voice of a critic—you are not what he says. You are what God says. **Isaiah 62:3** declares, *"You shall also be a crown of glory in the hand of the Lord."* You are loved, treasured, and seen. You may feel diminished, but you are not destroyed. God can restore your joy, rebuild your voice, and heal your heart.

To the man who recognizes his own critical spirit—there is hope. You can become a safe place, a source of joy, a wellspring of peace. But you must choose to change. You must ask the Holy Spirit to tame your tongue, soften your heart, and reprogram your reflexes. **Psalm 19:14** should become your prayer: *"Let the words of my mouth, and the meditation of my heart, be acceptable in your sight, O Lord."*

To the Church—may we stop celebrating harshness as strength. May we teach men that affirmation is not weakness that encouragement is not optional, and that love speaks life. Jesus was never critical toward those who came to Him in sincerity. Even the woman caught in adultery heard words of release, not rebuke: *"Neither do I condemn you: go, and sin no more"* **(John 8:11).** The critic would have stoned her. Jesus lifted her.

In a world where women are constantly bombarded with images and messages that challenge their worth, the voice of a husband should be a sanctuary—not a courtroom. A wise man knows that his wife's glow is not a coincidence—it is often a reflection of how he treats her. Let every husband learn the language of heaven: the language that builds, blesses, and believes.

Chapter 5

The Cheater, The Unfaithful Husband

Few betrayals sting the human soul like the wound of adultery. Infidelity is more than a sexual act—it is a deep violation of covenant, trust, and emotional safety. When a husband cheats, he does not merely sleep with another woman; he fractures the soul of the one he vowed to love, honor, and cherish. The cheater is a dangerous dude—not just because of what he does in the dark, but because of the ripple effect his unfaithfulness causes. His wife's confidence is shattered. Her self-worth is questioned. Her world is split between what she believed and what she now knows. The Bible does not take adultery lightly, nor should we.

In **Proverbs 6:32**, Scripture declares, *"Whoever commits adultery with a woman lacks understanding: he who does it destroys his own soul."* Adultery is not just foolish—it is self-destructive. It is a moral cancer that eats away at a man's integrity, his family structure, and his relationship with God. In a generation where sexual liberty is celebrated and commitment is treated as optional, the cheater hides behind cultural permissiveness while tearing his marriage apart. He lives a double life, often skilled at deception, yet oblivious to the destruction in his wake.

The devastation of adultery is vividly portrayed in the emotional, psychological, and spiritual trauma it causes the wife. She is left with a thousand questions that may never be answered: "Was I not enough?" "How long has this been going on?" "Was any of our love real?" Even when the infidelity is not physical—when it is emotional or pornographic—the betrayal runs deep. Jesus made no distinction between actual adultery and heart adultery when He said, *"Whoever looks at a woman to lust after her has committed adultery with her already in his heart"* **(Matthew 5:28).** Whether with a mistress, a screen, or a fantasy, the cheater betrays covenant.

The unfaithful husband often lives behind masks. He may appear spiritual, disciplined, or even romantic. But behind closed doors, he is addicted to self-gratification. His lust is insatiable. His conscience is seared. He may justify his behavior by pointing to his wife's imperfections, claiming she is too cold, too busy, or too distant. But these are excuses for a heart that has wandered. **James 1:14–15** lays the foundation: *"But every man is tempted, when he is drawn away by his own lust, and enticed. Then, when lust has conceived, it brings forth sin."* Adultery does not begin in the bed—it begins in the eyes and festers in the imagination.

The cheater may start with emotional distance—pulling away from his wife, becoming less interested in communication, avoiding spiritual intimacy. He becomes critical of her, irritated by her needs, and absent during vulnerable moments. Why? Because he is emotionally investing elsewhere. Many affairs begin long before physical contact ever happens. They start in text messages, flirtatious jokes, emotional dependencies, or harmless coffee chats that evolve into something much darker. **Song of Solomon 2:15** warns, *"Catch us the foxes, the little foxes, that spoil the vines."* Affairs often start with little foxes—small compromises that lead to complete betrayal.

Pornography, too, is a form of unfaithfulness. It violates the exclusivity of the marriage bed. **Hebrews 13:4** says, *"Marriage is honorable in all, and the bed undefiled: but whoremongers and* *adulterers God will judge."* When a man chooses digital images over the real, breathing woman he married, he fractures intimacy. His wife may not know right away, but her soul senses the disconnect. She feels the emotional unavailability, the shift in desire, the inattentiveness to her needs. The screen becomes the other woman—one who demands nothing but slowly steals everything.

Cheating is not just a private sin—it is a covenant breach. **Malachi 2:14–16** makes this clear: *"The Lord has been witness between you and the wife of your youth, against whom you have dealt treacherously... Therefore take heed to your spirit, and let none deal treacherously against the wife of his youth. For the Lord, the God of Israel, says that he hates putting away."* God Himself witnesses the betrayal. He does not stand neutral. He defends the brokenhearted and holds the unfaithful accountable. To cheat is to deal treacherously with God and with the woman He entrusted to one's care.

One of the most heartbreaking aspects of adultery is the loss of safety. Marriage is meant to be the safest place in a woman's life. But when a man cheats, he turns the home into a warzone of suspicion, fear, and brokenness. The wife is no longer able to rest emotionally. Every time he is late, every call he takes in another room, every sudden change in routine becomes a trigger. She becomes an investigator, forced to live in paranoia. This emotional turmoil is not punishment—it is trauma. The cheater has become a source of pain rather than protection.

Some cheaters repent only when caught. Their remorse is not for the sin but for the consequences. They are sorry because they were exposed, not because they broke trust. True repentance, however, is brokenness before God and the wife. **Psalm 51:17** reveals what God desires: *"The sacrifices of God are a broken spirit: a broken and a contrite heart, O God, you will not despise."* A truly repentant husband doesn't blame, doesn't shift responsibility, and doesn't expect instant forgiveness. He grieves over the wound he has caused and patiently rebuilds trust one day at a time.

Adultery is also a gateway for demonic torment. The cheater opens spiritual doors not only for himself but for his entire household. **Proverbs 7** paints a haunting picture of the adulteress, but the principle applies both ways. **Verse 27** says, *"Her house is the way to hell, going down to the chambers of death."* Sexual sin is never without spiritual consequence. It invites shame, confusion, and demonic interference. Many families battling depression, financial ruin, or division don't realize the origin was a hidden act of adultery that introduced a curse into the bloodline.

Children are not immune to the effects either. They may not know all the details, but they sense the coldness, the tension, and the unspoken sorrow between their parents. Sons grow up believing that faithfulness is optional. Daughters begin to question their worth. The example set by a cheating father creates generational patterns of betrayal unless repentance and deliverance are sought. Exodus 34:7 speaks of the iniquity of the fathers being visited upon the children and the children's children. A cheater isn't just hurting his wife—he's corrupting his legacy.

Yet amid the devastation, the Gospel offers hope. Even adulterers are not beyond redemption. David, a man after God's own heart, fell into the depths of adultery and murder (2 Samuel 11). Yet his sincere repentance in **Psalm 51** shows us the pathway to restoration: *"Create in me a clean heart, O God; and renew a right spirit within me"* **(v. 10)**. The cheater who turns to God in true brokenness can be forgiven. He can rebuild his marriage—but only if he commits to full transparency, lasting change, and the lifelong work of rebuilding shattered trust.

For the wife who has been cheated on, healing is possible, but it is not easy. Her world has been turned upside down. Her emotions will fluctuate. One day she may feel strong; the next, she may feel shattered. She must be given the space to grieve, to process, and to express her pain without being rushed into forgiveness. **Isaiah 61:3** speaks of giving those who mourn *"beauty for ashes, the oil of joy for* *mourning."* Healing is not linear, but God is near every step of the way.

Some wives choose to stay and work through the betrayal. Others choose to leave, especially in cases of ongoing unrepentant adultery. Both decisions can be biblically valid. Jesus allowed for divorce in cases of sexual unfaithfulness (Matthew 19:9). The church must support women, not pressure them into staying in unsafe or dishonorable conditions. God values covenant, but He also values the well-being of His daughters.

For the man who has cheated and desires restoration, he must understand that grace is not a free pass—it is an invitation to transformation. He must cut off all contact with the other woman, confess every detail without minimizing, seek godly counsel, undergo accountability, and be willing to walk through the valley of consequence without demanding immediate reconciliation. Trust broken takes time to rebuild. It is like shattered glass—possible to restore, but only with care, patience, and commitment.

Rebuilding involves a complete reorientation of character. The cheater must learn to walk in integrity, speak with transparency, and love sacrificially. **Ephesians 5:25** again becomes the standard: *"Husbands, love your wives, just as Christ loved the church and gave himself for it."* Christ did not cheat. He did not flirt with other gods. He was faithful even unto death. That is the standard of love the husband is called to imitate.

Sexual discipline must also become a priority. The cheater must not only avoid other women—he must starve the fantasy world that gave birth to betrayal. **Job 31:1** says, *"I made a covenant with my eyes; why then should I think upon a maid?"* The war for purity begins in the imagination. He must eliminate pornography, lust-filled media, inappropriate friendships, and seductive environments. He must fast, pray, and crucify his flesh daily. Lust must be starved—not entertained.

The cheater must also become emotionally available. Many men cheat because they have never developed the capacity for deep emotional connection. Rather than confront their inner void, they seek excitement elsewhere. But healing requires going inward. It requires facing childhood trauma, unhealed wounds, and toxic masculinity that equates love with conquest. **Proverbs 4:23** commands, *"Keep your heart with all diligence; for out of it spring the issues of life."* A faithful man is not just a loyal body—he is a steward of his heart.

The church must stop excusing adultery. We must not coddle cheaters because they are gifted, prominent, or male. God is not impressed by sermons if the preacher is sleeping around. **Malachi 2:17** says, *"You have wearied the Lord with your words."* He is weary of lip service without heart purity. The pulpit must uphold the sanctity of marriage with fear and trembling. Leaders must model fidelity—not just publicly, but privately.

To the wife betrayed: your pain is valid. Your tears are seen. Your identity is not defined by his betrayal. You are still beautiful. Still valuable. Still chosen. **Psalm 147:3** says, *"He heals the broken in heart, and binds up their wounds."* Let God be your refuge. Whether you stay or go, He will be with you.

To the man who has cheated: there is still time to change. You can become a man of honor. But it will require full surrender. No more secrets. No more double lives. No more blaming your wife. The prodigal must come home, not just to the house—but to the heart of God.

And to every marriage: guard your gates. Talk often. Pray daily. Make intimacy intentional. Protect your covenant fiercely. Adultery doesn't begin with sex—it begins with neglect. The cheater may have broken something precious, but with God, broken things can be made new.

CHAPTER 6

The Addict, Substance and Sexual Bondage

There is a certain kind of man whose presence in a marriage slowly erodes safety, love, and stability—not because he is violent or loud, but because he is ruled by cravings. His body is at home, but his soul is imprisoned. His loyalty is not to his wife or children, but to a bottle, a pill, a screen, a high, or an orgasm. He is the addict. Whether bound to alcohol, drugs, pornography, gambling, or sexual compulsions, this man is a dangerous dude. His addiction consumes not only his life but the emotional infrastructure of the entire household. Marriage becomes a battlefield of false promises, cycles of relapse, and unbearable isolation.

The addict is a man torn in two. On one side, he may genuinely love his wife and desire to be present. On the other, he is mastered by a habit so powerful that it overrides reason, love, and even fear. The apostle Paul describes this torment in **Romans 7:19:** *"For the good that I would, I do not: but the evil which I would not, that I do."* Addiction is not just a behavior—it is bondage. And bondage always affects more than the bound.

When a man is addicted, his wife is not simply a spouse—she becomes a hostage to his dysfunction. She must learn to manage chaos, cover shame, and absorb emotional fallout. Trust becomes impossible because promises are constantly broken. "This is the last time," he says. But it never is. **Proverbs 25:28** compares such a man to a city without walls: *"He who has no rule over his own spirit is like a city that is broken down, and without walls."* Without self-control, the addict becomes vulnerable to every temptation, every deception, and every demonic assault.

Addiction is a spiritual issue. It may manifest physically or psychologically, but its root is often found in the soul. It begins as a coping mechanism—a way to numb pain, escape stress, or feel powerful in the face of inadequacy. But what starts as a comfort quickly becomes a controller. In **John 8:34**, Jesus says, *"Whoever commits sin is the servant of sin."* Addiction enslaves. It steals identity, compromises integrity, and deforms intimacy. A husband addicted to lust, alcohol, or drugs cannot fully give himself to his wife. He is fragmented. He is hiding.

Substance abuse is particularly damaging in marriage because it alters the addict's behavior, personality, and ability to engage. A man under the influence of alcohol or drugs becomes unpredictable. He may be charming one moment and enraged the next. The wife learns to walk on eggshells. She may try to clean up after his mistakes—physically, emotionally, financially—hoping that he will "come back" to the man she once knew. But he is never fully there. **Proverbs 20:1** warns, *"Wine is a mocker, strong drink is raging: and whoever is deceived thereby is not wise."* Addiction mocks stability. It rages against peace. It leaves women weeping and children fatherless in spirit.

Sexual addiction, including pornography and compulsive masturbation, is just as destructive. The addict in sexual bondage often lives a double life—spiritual in public, sinful in secret. He may attend church, lead worship, or quote Scripture, but at home, he is glued to a screen, lost in fantasies, or trapped in endless cycles of shame. **Matthew 6:24** makes it clear: *"No man can serve two masters."* A man cannot serve his wife while serving his sexual cravings. Sooner or later, one master will dominate.

Pornography is not harmless entertainment—it is soul corrosion. It reshapes the brain, deadens sensitivity to real connection, and objectifies women. It replaces the sacred with the profane. **Ephesians 5:3** warns, *"But fornication, and all uncleanness... let it not be once named among you, as becomes saints."* Yet many men justify their use, calling it "normal," "natural," or even "a private struggle." But there is no such thing as private sin in marriage. What affects one affects both. A wife may not see the browser history, but she feels the distance, the disinterest, the dulling of intimacy.

Sexual addiction also leads to physical infidelity. Many men who start with pornography eventually seek escalation—chat rooms, webcams, prostitutes, or affairs. Sin, like fire, is never satisfied. **Proverbs 27:20** declares, *"Hell and destruction are never full; so the eyes of man are never satisfied."* The addicted man is always seeking a fix—more stimulation, more novelty, more excitement. But the thrill is always fleeting. And in its place come guilt, shame, and broken trust.

The wife of an addict suffers in silence. She often feels ashamed, wondering if she is the reason for his bondage. She may try to compete with the images he consumes or the substances he abuses. She wonders if her love is enough. But addiction is not a reflection of her inadequacy—it is a symptom of his brokenness. Her worth is not tied to his failure. **Isaiah 54:4** speaks directly to such women: *"Fear not; for you shall not be ashamed: neither be confounded; for you shall not be put to shame."* Her healing is not dependent on his repentance—though it is greatly helped by it.

Addiction also devastates finances. The addicted husband may drain savings, steal from accounts, or make irrational purchases to support his habit. The family suffers not just emotionally but economically. Bills go unpaid, debt increases, and future plans collapse. **1 Timothy 5:8** warns, *"But if anyone does not provide for his own... he has denied the faith, and is worse than an unbeliever."* A man ruled by addiction abandons his role as provider, protector, and priest.

There is also the erosion of spiritual leadership. An addicted man cannot lead his home in prayer, because his conscience is defiled. He may avoid devotion, withdraw from church, or fake spirituality to avoid exposure. But spiritual authority requires purity. **James 5:16** declares, *"The effectual fervent prayer of a righteous man avails much."* Addiction silences the voice of intercession and corrupts the flow of divine wisdom. A wife longing for spiritual partnership finds herself spiritually orphaned.

What, then, is the path to deliverance? The first step is confession. No man can conquer what he won't confront. **Proverbs 28:13** promises, *"He who covers his sins shall not prosper: but whoever confesses and forsakes them shall have mercy."* Addiction thrives in secrecy. Light breaks its power. The addicted man must tell the truth—to God, to his wife, to spiritual counsel. He must stop minimizing, blaming, and hiding. Healing begins with light.

Next is repentance—not remorse. Remorse feels bad but doesn't change. Repentance turns. It cuts ties with sin, makes no provision for relapse, and pursues radical transformation. **Romans 13:14** says, *"But put on the Lord Jesus Christ, and make no provision for the flesh."* The addicted man must throw away the alcohol, cancel the subscriptions, block the websites, delete the contacts, and submit himself to accountability.

Accountability is non-negotiable. Every addict needs spiritual covering and community. **James 5:16** commands, *"Confess your faults one to another, and pray for one another, that you may be healed."* Isolation breeds relapse. The man who truly wants freedom must humble himself under counsel, submit to mentoring, and receive correction. He must be willing to be monitored, questioned, and held responsible—not as punishment, but as protection.

Deliverance may also require professional help. Many addictions are rooted in trauma, childhood neglect, or mental health issues. Therapy, counseling, and support groups are not signs of weakness—they are pathways to wisdom. **Proverbs 11:14** says, *"In the multitude of counselors there is safety."* The man who rejects help remains in bondage. The man who embraces help begins to rebuild.

Spiritual warfare is essential. Addiction is not just a habit—it is a spiritual stronghold. **Ephesians 6:12** reminds us, *"For we wrestle not against flesh and blood... but against spiritual wickedness in high places."* Prayer, fasting, anointing, and deliverance ministry must be employed. The addicted man must learn to war in the Spirit. He must break covenants made with lust, addiction, and idolatry. He must evict every demon that entered through the open door of sin.

The process of restoration also includes restitution. The addicted husband must own the pain he caused. He must validate his wife's anger, grieve with her, and rebuild trust slowly. **Psalm 51:17** reveals God's posture: *"A broken and a contrite heart, O God, you will not despise."* The addicted man must embody brokenness—not perform it. His words must be backed by change. His apologies must be followed by action.

For the wife, healing is not passive. She must guard her heart, seek wise counsel, and set healthy boundaries. Forgiveness may be offered, but trust must be earned. Her emotional health must be prioritized. **Psalm 147:3** assures, *"He heals the broken in heart."* God is not only concerned with the addict—He is fiercely concerned with the woman wounded by him. She is not invisible. Her tears are not wasted.

Children, too, must be considered. Addiction destabilizes their sense of safety. Honest, age-appropriate conversations must be had. Counseling may be necessary. The goal is to stop the generational cycle. **Exodus 34:7** reminds us that iniquity can visit children *"to the third and fourth generation."* But that cycle can be broken by truth, healing, and intentional parenting.

The church must also rise in its role. We must no longer shame addicts into secrecy or coddle them into denial. We must preach freedom, walk in compassion, and provide resources for recovery. **Galatians**

6:1 instructs, *"If a man is overtaken in a fault, you who are spiritual, restore such a one in the spirit of meekness."* Restoration is the goal—but accountability is the road.

To the addict reading this—there is hope. You are not your addiction. You are not beyond saving. But you must make a decision. Will you continue to serve your cravings, or will you fall on your face before God? **Joel 2:13** says, *"Rend your heart, and not your garments, and turn to the Lord your God."* God is ready. The question is—are you?

To the wife of the addict—you are not alone. God is with you in the chaos. He sees the nights you cry yourself to sleep. He sees the effort you make to hold the family together. And He promises in **Psalm 34:18**, *"The Lord is near to those who are of a broken heart."* You are seen. You are loved. And you will not be forsaken.

To every marriage battling addiction—there is a way back. But it starts with truth, continues with surrender, and is sustained by grace. Let no man become so comfortable in sin that he forgets the sacredness of covenant. The addict may have fallen, but through Christ, he can rise.

CHAPTER 7

The Angry Man, Explosive and Unsafe

Of all the dangerous men a woman can marry, few bring as much terror into the home as the angry man. His anger does not need a reason—it simply needs a trigger. His temper lurks beneath the surface like a volcano, quiet one moment and erupting the next. The angry man is explosive, unpredictable, and unsafe. He transforms the marriage from a sanctuary into a minefield. His wife never knows what will set him off: a forgotten errand, a delayed meal, a child's mistake, a disagreement. She becomes hyper-vigilant, constantly trying to avoid the next outburst, but no amount of caution keeps her safe from the storm. His wrath is not discipline—it is destruction.

Proverbs 22:24–25 issues a dire warning: *"Make no friendship with an angry man; and with a furious man you shall not go: lest you learn his ways, and get a snare to your soul."* The angry man ensnares the soul of his wife. His rage does not correct—it corrupts. It trains the home in fear, silence, and self-preservation. His voice may not always be loud, but his presence is threatening. His emotions are a weapon, and his family walks through their days like prisoners of war—careful not to provoke their captor.

Anger itself is not sin. The Bible acknowledges anger as a human emotion. **Ephesians 4:26** says, *"Be angry, and do not sin: do not let* *the sun go down on your wrath.*" Jesus became angry when He saw injustice and hypocrisy (Mark 3:5). Righteous anger is controlled, purposeful, and temporary. But the angry man in this chapter is not experiencing righteous indignation. His anger is chronic, disproportionate, and unchecked. It is not a reaction—it is a lifestyle. He is not simply a man who gets angry—he is a man ruled by it.

The angry man often has a long history of unresolved pain. His explosions are not isolated—they are rooted. He may have grown up in a home filled with rage, where shouting and slamming doors were the norm. He may have experienced trauma, rejection, or emotional neglect. These unhealed wounds now manifest as fury. But instead of seeking healing, he demands submission. He punishes his wife for sins she did not commit. **Proverbs 14:17** declares, *"He who is soon angry deals foolishly."* The angry man makes foolish decisions, not just in arguments but in life. He ruins relationships, undermines trust, and destroys his own credibility.

In the early stages of the relationship, the angry man may not reveal his true nature. He might be intense, passionate, or "just emotional." His anger is often excused as masculinity or fire. He may even say, "I just care deeply," or "I'm just wired this way." But as the relationship progresses, the anger becomes more frequent, more severe, and more manipulative. The woman begins to realize that her opinions are not welcome, that any disagreement is seen as defiance, and that emotional safety is nonexistent.

The angry man thrives on control. His outbursts are not just emotional releases—they are tools of domination. When he yells, slams doors, breaks things, or drives recklessly, he is communicating one thing: "I am the power in this home." His wife may not be physically assaulted, but she is emotionally terrorized. She becomes small in his presence, not because she lacks strength, but because survival demands it. She avoids expressing needs, avoids asking questions, avoids "triggering" him. This is not submission—it is subjugation.

Anger can also be subtle. Not all angry men shout. Some use simmering silence, contemptuous glares, or biting sarcasm. These forms of passive-aggressive rage are just as damaging. They make the home cold, unsafe, and unpredictable. The wife never knows whether she will be met with affection or aggression. She cannot plan for the emotional climate of her day, because her husband's mood dictates everything.

The effects on children in such a home are profound. They learn early how to read emotional danger. They learn to hide, to lie, or to deflect blame. Boys growing up under an angry father often become either angry themselves or emotionally detached. Girls growing up in that environment may develop anxiety, low self-worth, or an unhealthy tolerance for future abuse. Ephesians 6:4 warns, "Fathers, do not provoke your children to wrath." Yet the angry man, by his very demeanor, provokes constantly—provoking fear, confusion, and bitterness.

Spiritually, the angry man cannot lead well. **James 1:20** makes it plain: *"For the wrath of man does not produce the righteousness of God."* His anger may win arguments, but it does not win hearts. He may demand submission, but he does not inspire trust. True leadership in marriage is not forceful—it is sacrificial. Christ is the model. He washed feet, held children, wept with friends, and laid down His life. He never exploded on the disciples. Even in righteous indignation, He was measured. The angry husband, in contrast, wants control without character, respect without relationship.

A common tactic of the angry man is blame-shifting. After an outburst, he may say things like, "You made me do it," or "If you hadn't pushed me, I wouldn't have reacted that way." This is manipulation. It denies accountability and places the responsibility for his emotions on his wife or children. It is the ancient lie of Adam, who said to God, *"The woman whom you gave to be with me, she gave me of the tree"* **(Genesis 3:12).** The angry man is always the victim, never the perpetrator.

What makes anger particularly dangerous is that it escalates. It often begins with raised voices and ends in broken furniture—or broken bodies. Many domestic violence cases begin with emotional and verbal abuse. The angry man may swear he would never hit his wife, but he slams walls, throws objects, or grabs in fits of rage. This is violence in embryo. And where it is allowed to grow, it will eventually explode. **Proverbs 15:18** warns, *"A wrathful man stirs up strife."* He is a magnet for drama, chaos, and pain.

To the wife of the angry man: You are not responsible for his anger. You are neither the cause nor the cure. His rage is his own responsibility. While forgiveness is godly, enabling abuse is not. **1 Corinthians 13:5** states that love *"is not easily provoked."* If he is constantly provoked, he is not walking in love. He needs help, deliverance, and accountability. You need safety, support, and clarity. Staying silent will not stop the storm. Rage never retires itself—it must be confronted.

Churches must do better in addressing this issue. Too often, women are told to "submit more," "pray harder," or "keep the home together," while the angry husband faces no correction. But God's standard is higher. **Malachi 2:16** says, *"For the Lord, the God of Israel, says that He hates divorce, for one covers violence with his garment."* God hates divorce—but He also hates the abuse that leads to it. Covering a man's anger because he is "spiritual" or "a provider" is not biblical—it is complicity.

There is hope for the angry man, but only through true repentance. He must stop making excuses, stop blaming others, and face the condition of his soul. **Proverbs 16:32** says, *"He who is slow to anger is better than the mighty, and he who rules his spirit than he who takes a city."* Anger management is not just about techniques—it is about transformation. The angry man must submit his emotions to the cross. He must fast, pray, and seek counseling. He must develop emotional intelligence and learn to express feelings without fire.

Jesus can heal the angry heart. In Mark 5, the man possessed by a legion of demons lived in tombs, screamed night and day, and was uncontrollable. But after encountering Christ, the Bible says he was *"sitting, clothed, and in his right mind"* **(Mark 5:15).** Deliverance is possible. Even the most volatile man can be transformed, but it requires humility, accountability, and a willingness to surrender control.

The angry man must also develop tools for self-regulation. He must learn to pause before speaking, walk away when agitated, and communicate without hostility. **Proverbs 15:1** offers timeless wisdom: *"A soft answer turns away wrath, but grievous words stir up anger."* He must understand that volume does not equal authority and intimidation does not equal leadership. Real men are gentle. Jesus said in **Matthew 11:29**, *"Learn from me, for I am meek and lowly in heart."*

If you are the angry man reading these words, you have a choice. You can defend yourself or deliver yourself. You can harden your heart or humble it. But know this: if you continue in rage, you will destroy your marriage, your children, your health, and your soul. **Ecclesiastes 7:9** warns, *"Do not be hasty in your spirit to be angry, for anger rests in the bosom of fools."* Don't be a fool. Let God perform heart surgery before your rage ruins everything.

To the wife suffering under his anger: Seek safety. Do not spiritualize abuse. God does not want you to be a sacrifice on the altar of your husband's emotions. Seek counsel and set boundaries. If necessary, separate until change is proven. You are not less spiritual for protecting your peace. **Psalm 46:1** declares, *"God is our refuge and strength, a very present help in trouble."* Let Him be your shield.

Anger left unchecked becomes a generational curse. What we tolerate today, our children inherit tomorrow. Let the cycle end with this generation. Let the legacy shift from wrath to wisdom, from fear to faith, from violence to virtue.

In summary, the angry man is dangerous not only because of his actions but because of the atmosphere he creates: one of fear, silence, and instability. His transformation begins with self-awareness, continues through repentance, and is sustained by a renewed mind. **Romans 12:2** offers the key: *"Be transformed by the renewing of your mind."* If his mind can change, his words can change. If his words can change, his marriage can heal.

Chapter 8

The Passive Man, Present But Powerless

Not all dangerous men are loud, violent, or visibly abusive. Some are quiet, agreeable, and even charming—but deadly in their indecision and disengagement. These men don't explode with anger or betray with adultery; instead, they abandon through avoidance. They disappear behind smiles, television screens, hobbies, or spiritual-sounding detachment. They are not absent physically, but they are passive. They are present in the home but absent in the marriage. They avoid conflict, defer responsibility, and refuse to lead. They are not dangerous because of what they do—but because of what they refuse to do. They are the passive men—present but powerless.

Passivity is the subtle killer of many marriages. The passive man does not destroy his home with violence but with silence. His wife longs for leadership, but he shrinks back. She craves partnership, but he detaches. She pleads for spiritual direction, but he offers blank stares or vague spiritual clichés. **Proverbs 18:9** says, *"He who is slothful in his work is brother to him who is a great waster."* The passive man is the silent cousin of the abuser and the destroyer. He may not rage or cheat, but his passivity produces similar devastation. He fails to protect, guide, and cultivate the home, resulting in emotional abandonment and spiritual famine.

The first man in Scripture, Adam, models this type of passivity. In Genesis 3, when the serpent came to tempt Eve, Adam was right there—yet he said nothing. He watched the enemy deceive his wife and did not intervene. He did not protect, lead, or correct. He stood by, present but powerless. When God confronted him, Adam did not repent with responsibility; instead, he blamed both Eve and God: *"The woman whom you gave to be with me, she gave me of the tree, and I did eat"* **(Genesis 3:12).** Adam's sin was not just eating the fruit—it was his silence in the face of danger.

Today, many women are married to modern-day Adams. These men are physically in the home but emotionally and spiritually absent. They do not initiate meaningful conversations. They do not set spiritual direction. They make no real decisions. Their leadership is passive at best and nonexistent at worst. The wife becomes both mother and manager—making all the plans, carrying all the spiritual weight, and constantly trying to motivate her husband to engage. But the passive man sees leadership as optional, not essential.

The passive man is often a product of fear. He fears failure, so he avoids responsibility. He fears confrontation, so he chooses peacekeeping over peacemaking. He fears rejection, so he disengages. Yet the Bible makes it clear in **2 Timothy 1:7**, *"For God has not given us a spirit of fear, but of power, and of love, and of a sound mind."* Fear cannot be the guiding force of manhood. Passivity is not humility—it is cowardice dressed in politeness. God did not design men to fade into the background. He designed them to lead, to love, and to cover.

A passive husband often says, "Whatever you want, babe," not out of love but to avoid responsibility. He may avoid correcting his children when discipline is needed. He may avoid family decisions about finances, church attendance, or boundaries with extended family. He defers everything to his wife—not because she's more capable, but because he's afraid to carry the weight. This deference is not biblical submission—it is spiritual negligence.

Ephesians 5:23 says, *"For the husband is the head of the wife, as Christ is the head of the church."* Headship is not dictatorship—it is divine responsibility. Jesus did not avoid His bride. He washed her with the Word, fed her, died for her, and led her into glory. The passive man avoids spiritual responsibility, leaving his wife vulnerable. Without covering, she is exposed to emotional exhaustion, spiritual burnout, and decision fatigue. She was made to be a helper—not the hero.

Passivity also breeds resentment. The wife begins to feel like a single parent and solo believer—carrying everything while her husband scrolls his phone, buries himself in hobbies, or disappears into career obsession. Over time, admiration fades. Passion wanes. She stops looking to him for wisdom and starts looking inward or, worse, outward. The home becomes functional but emotionally dry. Conversations revolve around logistics, not love. Intimacy becomes a duty, not a delight. The wife withers, not because her husband is cruel, but because he is consistently disengaged.

The passive man may even hide behind spirituality. He may quote verses, say "God is in control," or delegate everything to divine timing—but in reality, he is using God-talk to mask his refusal to act. **James 2:17** says, *"Even so faith, if it has no works, is dead, being alone."* Real faith produces action. Godly men take initiative. They don't wait for their wives to beg for prayer, intimacy, or attention. They step up because love demands it.

The children of a passive father suffer deeply. Sons lack a model for godly manhood. They learn that masculinity means being agreeable but detached. Daughters, seeing their mother carry everything, may grow up believing they must do the same. Worse yet, the emotional vacuum left by a passive father can be filled by friends, media, or predators. **Proverbs 13:22** says, *"A good man leaves an inheritance to his children's children."* That inheritance must include emotional engagement and spiritual leadership—not just financial provision.

So why do some men choose passivity? Many were raised in homes where leadership was distorted. Perhaps their fathers were abusive, so they overcorrected into silence. Perhaps they were told, "Real men don't cry" or "Just let the woman have her way." Cultural confusion, poor modeling, and unresolved trauma all contribute. But Christ offers a new model. He shows that true strength is not found in avoiding responsibility but in embracing it.

The path to transformation begins with honesty. The passive man must admit his disengagement. He must face the fact that his silence is hurting his family. **Proverbs 27:17** says, *"Iron sharpens iron; so a man sharpens the countenance of his friend."* He must pursue mentorship, counseling, and community—not to become louder, but to become stronger. Leadership is not about volume—it's about vision.

Next comes intentional action. The passive man must develop the habit of initiation. This means initiating prayer, conversation, date nights, discipline, and dreams. He must show up—fully and consistently. **Joshua 24:15** provides the example: *"As for me and my house, we will serve the Lord."* Joshua didn't wait for a consensus. He declared, led, and lived his decision. The passive man must learn to speak like a man who believes his voice matters.

Passivity must also be replaced with presence. A godly man shows up emotionally. He listens attentively. He asks his wife how she's really doing and stays for the answer. He makes eye contact. He offers empathy. He does not shut down during conflict. He does not numb himself with food, media, or busyness. He leans in. **Psalm 34:15** assures us, *"The eyes of the Lord are upon the righteous, and His ears are open to their cry."* The godly man mirrors this attentiveness in his home.

Passivity is also conquered through courage. A man cannot lead well if he fears failure more than he values growth. He must be willing to make mistakes and learn from them. **Proverbs 24:16** says, *"For a just* *man falls seven times, and rises up again."* Leadership is not perfection—it's persistence. The passive man must become a man who rises, repents quickly, and walks forward even when afraid.

For the wife of a passive man: Your pain is real. You are not imagining the weight. You may feel like you are holding your entire family together while your husband hides. But you are not alone. God sees your labor, your prayers, and your tears. **Galatians 6:9** promises, *"Let us not be weary in well doing: for in due season we shall reap, if we faint not."* Stay faithful, but don't carry everything. Call your husband up into his role. Speak truth in love. Set boundaries. Invite him into counseling. You don't have to carry this forever.

To the church: Let us call men to rise. Let us preach courage, not control. Let us model leadership that serves, covers, and empowers. Let us train men not just to work hard at jobs, but to work hard at home. Headship is not about domination—it is about devotion.

To the passive man reading this: God is calling you out of hiding. Like Elijah in the cave, the Lord is asking, *"What are you doing here?"* **(1 Kings 19:9).** You were made for more. You are not weak—you are just untrained. But God is the ultimate Father. He will teach you how to love, lead, and live with strength. Rise up. Take your place. Speak. Act. Pray. Cover. Lead.

Passivity is not peace—it is the absence of war at the cost of victory. A family led by a passive man may avoid conflict for a while, but they also avoid growth. The marriage stagnates. The children drift. The home survives but never thrives.

Let every man reject the lie that "doing nothing" is harmless. In marriage, doing nothing when leadership is needed is doing damage. Let every husband say, "Not on my watch." Not on my watch will my wife carry the spiritual weight alone. Not on my watch will my children grow up leaderless. Not on my watch will silence speak louder than truth.

DEADLY DUDES

May the Spirit of God awaken every man who has fallen asleep at the wheel. May he rise, repent, and return—not just to the marriage, but to the mission. Let him once again become a man of presence, power, and prayer.

Chapter 9:

The Deceiver, Living a Lie

There is no greater threat to the sanctity of marriage than dishonesty. Lies—whether subtle or overt—are termites in the beams of trust. They weaken the very structure of intimacy, eroding confidence and sabotaging covenant. The deceiver is not always loud or abusive. He may be gentle in speech, generous with gifts, and convincing in his performance. But beneath the charm and polish lies a life built on half-truths, secret sins, and manipulation. The deceiver is a dangerous man because he violates the most sacred principle of marriage: truth.

The essence of a marital covenant is rooted in vulnerability. **Genesis 2:25** paints the ideal: *"And they were both naked, the man and his wife, and were not ashamed."* This speaks not only to physical nudity but to emotional transparency. True intimacy thrives where nothing is hidden. But the deceiver refuses transparency. He wears masks. He lives in layers. He tells his wife what she wants to hear while living what she must never know. He smiles in her presence while hiding secrets in her absence. His entire marriage is built on illusion.

A deceiver lives in a dual reality—what his wife sees and what she never suspects. He may hide an affair, a secret addiction, a financial double life, or a completely fabricated identity. He may pretend to be deeply spiritual while privately indulging in sin. He may lead in public but lie in private. **Proverbs 12:22** says, *"Lying lips are an abomination to the Lord, but those who deal truly are His delight."*

God does not merely dislike lying—He detests it. Yet the deceiver builds his entire existence around it.

Deception in marriage is uniquely evil because it violates trust on a covenantal level. Trust is the currency of intimacy. Without it, there is no safety, no joy, no unity. When a husband deceives his wife, he robs her of the ability to make informed decisions. He manipulates her emotions, redirects her expectations, and distorts her perception of reality. Over time, she begins to question her own judgment. She senses something is off but can't quite identify it. She feels disoriented, anxious, and increasingly insecure.

This form of betrayal is often called "gaslighting." Gaslighting is a form of psychological abuse where the deceiver intentionally causes the other person to question their memory, perception, or sanity. For instance, when a wife confronts her husband about suspicious behavior, he may respond with, "You're just imagining things," "You're too emotional," or "You're crazy." Over time, she stops trusting herself and relies entirely on the narrative the deceiver provides. This is a wicked manipulation of reality and a direct assault on her mental and emotional health.

One biblical example of a deceiver is Judas Iscariot. He traveled with Jesus, listened to His teachings, participated in miracles, and shared meals with Him—yet all the while, he was secretly plotting betrayal. **John 12:6** reveals that Judas, while pretending to care for the poor, was stealing from the ministry's funds. He looked like a disciple but lived like a deceiver. Similarly, many men live dual lives in their marriages. They play the part, speak the language, and even serve in ministry—but their hearts are divided, their stories fabricated, and their love false.

The deceiver is a master of appearances. He knows how to say the right things, offer timely apologies, and present himself as humble or misunderstood. But his sorrow is performative, not transformative. **2 Corinthians 7:10** distinguishes between the two: *"For godly sorrow* *produces repentance leading to salvation... but the sorrow of the world produces death."* The deceiver feels remorse only when caught, not when sinning. His confessions are strategic, his tears manipulative. His goal is not restoration but the preservation of his lies.

A deceiving husband often traps his wife in a cycle of confusion and apology. He may withdraw emotionally, then return with charm. He may deny wrongdoing until confronted with evidence, then pivot to emotional appeals. He may cry, beg, promise, and repent—all to buy time for his hidden life. These cycles are abusive, designed to reset the narrative while keeping her disoriented and submissive.

Lying also includes omission. A man does not need to tell outright falsehoods to be a deceiver. Withholding information, manipulating facts, or selectively sharing partial truths is equally destructive. **Ephesians 4:25** commands, *"Therefore, putting away lying, let each one of you speak truth with his neighbor, for we are members of one another."* In marriage, your spouse is not just your neighbor—she is your other self. To lie to her is to divide yourself.

Financial deception is another realm where many husbands live in secrecy. They may hide debt, maintain secret accounts, or gamble away resources while assuring their wives, "Everything's fine." This deceit is often justified as "protecting her from stress," but in reality, it is about control. It undermines unity and partnership. **Amos 3:3** asks, *"Can two walk together, unless they are agreed?"* Agreement requires truth. A deceiver cannot lead in unity because he walks in secrecy.

Sexual deception, including hidden pornography use, secret flirtations, or emotional affairs, is equally devastating. The man may claim he's "just chatting" or "just watching," but Jesus sets the standard: *"Whoever looks at a woman to lust after her has already committed adultery with her in his heart"* **(Matthew 5:28).** The deceiver does not protect his marriage bed—he pollutes it in silence.

The wife of a deceiver suffers deeply. She may not be able to prove the lies, but she senses them. Her intuition is constantly at war with the image her husband projects. She feels crazy, insecure, and unseen. She begins to question whether she is worthy of the truth. This emotional warfare leads to depression, anxiety, and isolation. **Psalm 55:12–14** captures her pain: *"For it was not an enemy that reproached me... but it was thou, a man mine equal, my guide, and mine acquaintance. We took sweet counsel together, and walked unto the house of God in company."* Betrayal by a spouse is uniquely painful because it breaks both heart and covenant.

Children growing up under deception learn to lie early. They see the duplicity and learn that survival requires silence. They may lose respect for both parents—the father for his lies and the mother for her passivity. The home becomes a theatre where everyone performs and no one heals. The generational impact is incalculable. **Psalm 101:7** says, *"He that worketh deceit shall not dwell within my house."* God has no tolerance for deception, and neither should we.

So how does the deceiver find deliverance? It begins with brutal honesty. **Proverbs 28:13** says, *"He that covereth his sins shall not prosper: but whoso confesseth and forsaketh them shall have mercy."* True repentance is not just confession—it is forsaking. The deceiver must come completely clean. No more partial truths. No more selective memory. No more blame-shifting. Every lie must be exposed. Every secret surrendered.

Restoration requires accountability. The deceiver must submit to pastoral care, spiritual mentorship, and possibly professional counseling. He must give his wife full access to his digital life, his finances, and his communications—not as a prisoner, but as a partner seeking trust. Trust, once broken, is not restored by words—but by consistent, proven transparency over time.

Deliverance also requires spiritual warfare. Deception is not just a habit—it is often a stronghold. The devil is the *"father of lies"* **(John**

8:44), and every deceiver carries his signature. Only through the power of the Holy Spirit can a man be truly freed from compulsive lying. He must fast, pray, and submit to deliverance ministry. He must hate his sin more than he fears exposure. Only then can he walk in truth.

To the wife living with a deceiver—you are not crazy. Your intuition is valid. Your longing for truth is righteous. You deserve honesty, clarity, and consistency. You do not have to settle for half-truths and hollow apologies. If your husband refuses to come clean, refuses to seek help, and continues to manipulate, you have every biblical right to confront, to separate, and to seek wise counsel. God is not asking you to suffer in a house of mirrors.

To the church—stop celebrating charm over character. Stop giving platforms to gifted men who live in hidden sin. God is calling for purity in leadership, transparency in marriage, and truth in every relationship. The cost of looking the other way is too great.

To the man reading this, who recognizes himself in these paragraphs—this is your call to repentance. No more lies. No more silence. No more secrets. Come into the light. Confess. Repent. Rebuild. God can restore what you've destroyed, but only if you stop pretending. Psalm 51:6 declares, "Behold, thou desirest truth in the inward parts." God doesn't want your performance—He wants your honesty.

And finally, to every marriage battling deception: know this—truth is your only road back to intimacy. Lies may buy temporary peace, but only truth can build eternal trust. Choose truth. Choose light. Choose freedom.

CHAPTER 10

The Silent Abuser, When the Wounds Are Invisible

Abuse is often imagined as bruises, broken furniture, and emergency calls. It is typically associated with screaming matches, raised fists, or hospital visits. But not all abuse leaves a mark on the skin. Some wounds go undetected, hidden beneath smiles and Sunday best. They bleed inwardly—quietly. The one inflicting them is not always raging, violent, or intoxicated. He may be calm, soft-spoken, and even admired in the community. Yet behind closed doors, he is an expert at cutting with silence, shaming with indifference, and suffocating with neglect. He is the silent abuser—a dangerous man whose tools of control are invisible but no less violent.

Emotional and psychological abuse is one of the most misunderstood and underrecognized forms of abuse in marriage. It doesn't make headlines. It doesn't show up in physical exams. It leaves no bruises on the body—but it breaks the soul. **Proverbs 18:14** speaks to this internal devastation: *"The spirit of a man will sustain his infirmity, but a wounded spirit who can bear?"* When a man wounds his wife with prolonged silence, detachment, manipulation, and emotional withholding, he slowly breaks her spirit. And often, no one else even knows.

DEADLY DUDES

The silent abuser does not shout—he withdraws. He does not strike—he withholds. He may never call his wife names, but he starves her of warmth, intimacy, and connection. His tools are silence, avoidance, dismissiveness, passive-aggression, stonewalling, and emotional coldness. He uses these not out of ignorance but as instruments of control. His wife is left constantly second-guessing herself, wondering what she did wrong. She becomes a prisoner in a relationship where communication is weaponized and affection is rationed.

Unlike physical abuse, silent abuse is easy to disguise. The husband may appear polite in public, spiritual in church, and even charming at family gatherings. But at home, he gives his wife the cold shoulder for days after a disagreement. He refuses to discuss issues, retreating into silence that punishes. He may withhold sex, praise, or simple conversation—not as an act of distance but as an act of power. **Proverbs 27:15** warns, *"A continual dripping on a rainy day and a contentious woman are alike."* Yet the silent abuser creates the very contention he then blames her for. His wife's frustration is treated as instability when it is actually a cry for connection.

This kind of abuse can take many forms. One is emotional neglect—the failure to show empathy, concern, or genuine interest in his wife's thoughts and feelings. The silent abuser is emotionally unavailable and disinterested. His wife may pour out her heart only to be met with blank stares, distracted responses, or total indifference. He may change the subject, scroll his phone, or walk away mid-sentence. This communicates one message repeatedly: "You don't matter."

Another form is gaslighting, where he makes his wife question her perception of reality. If she expresses concern about his behavior, he denies it happened or accuses her of being too sensitive. If she brings up neglect, he blames her for imagining things. Over time, she begins to believe she is the problem. This tactic is strategic, keeping her insecure, confused, and dependent. **Psalm 55:21** captures this tactic well: *"The words of his mouth were smoother than butter, but war was in his heart."*

The silent abuser is often deeply insecure. His need for control stems from a fear of vulnerability. He avoids confrontation not because he's peace-loving, but because he is manipulative. By refusing to talk, he maintains the upper hand. He controls the emotional temperature of the home—not through shouting, but through silence. His presence becomes a constant reminder that love must be earned and peace is always conditional.

This form of abuse often includes spiritual manipulation. The silent abuser may weaponize Scripture to maintain dominance. He might quote verses about submission while ignoring his duty to love sacrificially. He may refuse to pray with his wife or attend church together, yet still expect to be treated as the head of the home. This creates a spiritual imbalance that starves the marriage. **Ephesians 5:25** says, *"Husbands, love your wives, as Christ also loved the church and gave Himself for it."* The silent abuser gives nothing. He only takes.

Intimacy also suffers tremendously. In many cases, the silent abuser withholds physical affection or sexual intimacy—not due to emotional distance, but as a deliberate tool of punishment. This violates **1 Corinthians 7:5**, which says, *"Do not deprive one another, except with consent for a time."* Marriage is meant to be a place of mutual pleasure and emotional safety. But the silent abuser turns it into a place of cold obligation or emotional rejection.

The long-term effects on the wife are devastating. She begins to lose her sense of identity. She questions her worth, her intuition, and her sanity. She may develop depression, anxiety, or chronic fatigue. The stress of living in an emotionally unpredictable environment erodes her health. She smiles in public but cries in private. She becomes emotionally exhausted, spiritually dry, and relationally numb. Because the abuse is silent, she often feels alone in her suffering.

Children in the home are not unaffected. They sense the coldness. They notice the lack of affection, the forced smiles, and the tension that fills the air. Sons may grow up emotionally shut down, believing that masculinity means distance. Daughters may normalize emotional unavailability, believing that love must be earned through perfection. **Psalm 127:3** calls children *"a heritage from the Lord,"* but the silent abuser passes down dysfunction rather than blessing.

How does the silent abuser justify his behavior? Many believe they are avoiding conflict. "I don't like drama," they say. Others claim moral superiority: "She's the emotional one—I'm just calm." But avoidance is not a virtue. It is a form of control. A refusal to engage is not peaceful—it is passive-aggressive warfare. **James 4:17** says, *"To him who knows to do good and does not do it, to him it is sin."* The silent abuser sins not by what he says, but by what he refuses to say.

Church culture often enables the silent abuser. Because he may not be visibly angry or adulterous, he is rarely confronted. He appears "quiet" and "non-confrontational," which is mistaken for gentleness. Meanwhile, his wife is seen as "emotional" or "hard to please." But Jesus said in **John 8:32**, *"You shall know the truth, and the truth shall make you free."* Emotional silence in marriage is a lie. It says, "There is peace," when there is none. It must be exposed for what it is—abuse.

What is the way forward for the silent abuser? It begins with recognition. He must acknowledge that silence can be as harmful as shouting, that avoidance is not love, and that withholding affection, ignoring concerns, and refusing communication are all forms of abuse. **Proverbs 27:6** says, *"Faithful are the wounds of a friend; but the kisses of an enemy are deceitful."* The silent abuser wounds with his silence while pretending to love with his composure. He must repent.

Repentance includes confession—not just to God, but to his wife. He must admit the emotional damage he has caused. He must ask specific questions: "How have I made you feel unseen?" "When have I made you feel alone?" And then—he must listen. Not defend. Not dismiss.

Just listen. Proverbs 18:13 warns, *"He who answers a matter before he hears it, it is folly and shame to him."* Healing begins with humility.

Next, he must pursue emotional discipleship. This may include counseling, reading, accountability, and prayer. He must learn how to feel, how to express, and how to lead emotionally. He must stop retreating into passivity and begin showing up in vulnerability. **Romans 12:15** commands, *"Rejoice with those who rejoice, and weep with those who weep."* A godly husband engages with his wife's emotions. He does not escape them.

For the wife: Your pain is valid. You are not imagining it. You are not being "too sensitive." You are living in a form of abuse that many don't recognize—but God sees it. **Psalm 34:18** promises, *"The Lord is near to those who have a broken heart."* Seek counseling. Speak the truth. Refuse to be gaslighted into silence. You were created to be loved, not just tolerated.

If safety permits, confront the silence. Say what you see. Ask the hard questions. If there is no change, consider a mediated separation to establish clarity and boundaries. Do not accept coldness as normal. God's design for marriage includes affection, transparency, and shared emotional weight.

To pastors and leaders: Teach about emotional abuse. Preach against silence that harms. Counsel husbands to speak, listen, and engage. Don't just condemn loud sins—confront the silent sins that destroy from within.

To the man who recognizes himself in these words: Today can be your turning point. You can become a man who is emotionally present, spiritually sensitive, and relationally safe. God does not want a polished exterior—He wants your heart. **Ezekiel 36:26** declares, *"A new heart also will I give you, and a new spirit will I put within you."* Let Him make you new.

DEADLY DUDES

The silent abuser may not leave bruises, but he breaks hearts. He erodes connection. He mocks covenant by making love conditional. But love is not cold. Love is not silent. Love speaks, listens, touches, and stays. Let the silent man find his voice—not to control, but to connect.

May every home once frozen by silence thaw in the warmth of truth. May every wife once ignored be seen. May every husband once disengaged rise to become the man who not only stands in the room but speaks life into it.

CHAPTER 11

The Mama's Boy, Married to His Mother

There is a kind of man whose greatest loyalty is not to his wife but to his mother. Though he wears a wedding band and has made vows before God and man, his heart remains tethered to the apron strings of the woman who raised him. His allegiance is split. His authority is compromised. His marriage suffers—not from infidelity with another woman, but from emotional fusion with the one who birthed him. He is the mama's boy—a dangerous man cloaked in gentleness, but destructive in his divided loyalties. He is not fully married to his wife because he is still emotionally married to his mother.

The biblical mandate for marriage is unambiguous. **Genesis 2:24** declares, *"Therefore shall a man leave his father and his mother, and shall cleave unto his wife: and they shall be one flesh."* The Hebrew word for "leave" is *azab*, which means to forsake, abandon, or relinquish. It does not mean to dishonor—but to detach. A man cannot truly cleave until he has first left. The man who remains emotionally tied to his mother undermines the unity of his home before it ever begins.

The mama's boy never truly left. He may have moved into a new house, started a new life, and gone through the ceremony of marriage—but in his soul, he remains under his mother's governance.

She still calls the shots. She influences his decisions. She competes with his wife for attention, affection, and influence. In some cases, she disrespects or overrides his wife—and he says nothing. He becomes passive toward his wife but protective toward his mother. The triangle is clear: his wife married him, but he remains married to his mother.

This dynamic creates emotional chaos in the marriage. The wife feels like a second-class citizen. She is expected to build a home, bear children, and support her husband—but she is not allowed first place in his heart. Every disagreement becomes a three-way struggle. If she challenges him, she risks him running to his mother for validation. If she sets boundaries, she is labeled controlling. If she asks for space from his family, she is called divisive. The wife of a mama's boy lives in a constant state of emotional compromise—trying to build a marriage with a man who still belongs to someone else.

In Scripture, we find an example of this dynamic in the life of Rebekah and her son Jacob. Rebekah, though a godly woman in many respects, inserted herself into the affairs of her sons—especially Jacob—using manipulation and deceit to secure his blessing (Genesis 27). While her motive may have been theological, her methods sowed division between Jacob and Esau for years. A mother who refuses to let go of her adult son may cloak her actions in love, but at the root is often fear, pride, or control.

The mama's boy may not realize how destructive this dynamic is. He may justify his actions by saying, "She's just helping," "She means well," or "That's just how she is." But his wife hears a different message: "You're not my priority." A man who refuses to establish boundaries with his mother dishonors both women. He creates a divided kingdom where loyalty is constantly questioned, and intimacy cannot flourish. **Matthew 12:25** says, *"Every kingdom divided against itself is brought to desolation."* A marriage without clear boundaries is a divided kingdom—and it will not stand.

The mother-son bond is sacred, but it must evolve. Healthy mothers understand that raising a son includes preparing him to leave. They release him with blessing, not bitterness. But unhealthy mothers guilt their sons into staying emotionally tethered. They may use illness, financial entanglement, or emotional appeals to keep their sons close. **Proverbs 22:6** is often quoted to parents: *"Train up a child in the way he should go."* But the second part of that verse implies letting go when he's older. Training a son includes preparing him to prioritize his future family, not his family of origin.

When a man fails to make this shift, he confuses honor with allegiance. **Ephesians 6:2** says, *"Honor your father and mother."* But honor is not the same as obedience. Honor is respect; obedience is compliance. Once a man marries, his first allegiance is to his wife—not his mother. If his mother demands compliance over boundaries, she is requiring something that violates the marriage covenant. A godly man must honor his mother while protecting his marriage.

The mama's boy also struggles with autonomy. He may have never learned to make decisions without his mother's approval. He may seek her opinion on everything—from financial matters to parenting—often over his wife's perspective. This erodes his wife's sense of value and influence. She becomes a resident, not a partner. **Proverbs 31:11** describes a woman whose *"husband safely trusts in her."* A man who trusts his mother more than his wife violates the sacred balance of that trust.

In some cases, the mother-in-law openly undermines the wife. She may criticize her cooking, parenting, or housekeeping. She may insert herself into disagreements or act as if her son is still single. The mama's boy rarely defends his wife. He may say, "That's just how she is," or, "Don't be so sensitive." But failing to defend his wife is betrayal by silence. **1 Peter 3:7** commands husbands to *"dwell with them according to knowledge, giving honor to the wife."* Honoring your wife means standing up for her—even to your mother.

The spiritual consequences of this dynamic are profound. The marriage becomes spiritually stagnant. The husband is unable to lead because he is emotionally divided. His wife cannot flourish because she is emotionally diminished. Prayer life is strained. Intimacy is stifled. Communication becomes a minefield. And Satan exploits the breach. Where there is division, the enemy has a foothold.

The children in such a marriage also suffer. They grow up witnessing divided authority. Sons may become confused about their father's role. Daughters may fear marriage, believing that being a wife means always coming second. The legacy of dysfunction is passed on, not through words but through example. **Exodus 20:5** warns that iniquity is *"visited upon the children unto the third and fourth generation."* A man must choose whether he will repeat the past or break the cycle.

So what is the path forward for the mama's boy? It begins with courageous detachment. He must recognize that emotional allegiance to his mother is no longer appropriate. This doesn't mean cutting her off but repositioning her. She is no longer his primary confidant, decision-maker, or emotional anchor—his wife is. He must say, like Joshua, *"As for me and my house, we will serve the Lord"* **(Joshua 24:15)**—not mama.

Next comes boundary setting. This includes limiting conversations about marital issues with his mother, refusing to tolerate dishonor toward his wife, and ensuring his wife feels prioritized in family interactions. Boundaries are not rebellion—they are protection. Even Jesus, when told by His mother that His time had come, said, *"Woman, what have I to do with you? My hour has not yet come"* **(John 2:4)**. Jesus knew how to honor without compromising His assignment.

The husband must also work on emotional maturation. He must develop independence in thought, decision-making, and spiritual leadership. He must stop leaning on his mother and start leading his home. **1 Corinthians 13:11** says, "When I became a man, I put away childish things." Clinging to mommy is a childish thing. True manhood requires emotional separation and spiritual ownership.

To the wife married to a mama's boy: You are not unreasonable for wanting to be first. God designed marriage to be exclusive. You are not second. You are not the enemy. You are his God-ordained helper and covenant partner. Do not internalize rejection as worthlessness. Instead, speak the truth in love. Set healthy boundaries. Invite your husband into honest conversation. But also remember: you cannot force a man to grow up. He must choose to.

To mothers: Release your sons. Do not sabotage their marriages with your nostalgia, fear, or control. Celebrate your son's new life. Bless his wife. Stay in your role. You are still honored, but you are no longer first. That's not rejection—it's God's order.

To pastors and leaders: Teach men to leave and cleave. Don't just preach about submission—preach about separation from parental control. Equip families to set boundaries without shame. Don't spiritualize dysfunction—break it with truth.

To the man reading this: If you are a mama's boy, it's time to grow up. Your mother raised you—thank her, honor her, love her. But do not let her sabotage your home. Your wife deserves all of you, not what's left after your mother takes her share. Break the soul tie. Draw the boundary. Take your place as protector, provider, and priest—not of your mother's house, but your own.

CHAPTER 12

The Hypocrite, Double Life, Double Standard

Of all the roles a man can play in the breakdown of his marriage, none is more insidious than that of the hypocrite. He is not the angry man who shouts, the violent man who strikes, or the cheater who strays. Instead, he is the man who pretends—who lives one way in public and another at home. He is often admired by outsiders, praised in religious or social circles, and seen as a man of integrity. But his wife knows a different version. In public, he is pious; in private, he is passive or perverse. In church, he's respected; at home, he's resented. His words are righteous, but his ways are rotten. This man is the hypocrite—a dangerous man who hides behind appearances while destroying trust behind closed doors.

Hypocrisy is not just a flaw; it is a lifestyle of contradiction. The Greek word *hypokritēs* means "actor"—someone who wears a mask. The hypocrite is skilled at performance. He knows what to say, how to behave, and which Scriptures to quote. But his religion is a costume. He honors God with his lips, but his heart is far from Him (Matthew 15:8). He leads worship, preaches sermons, gives generously, or volunteers in service, but at home, he is cold, emotionally unavailable, impatient, selfish, or even abusive. His hypocrisy is not a moment of weakness—it is a double life.

Jesus had strong words for such men. In Matthew 23, He confronted the religious leaders who looked godly but lived corruptly: *"Woe to you, scribes and Pharisees, hypocrites! For you are like whitewashed tombs, which indeed appear beautiful outwardly, but inside are full of dead men's bones"* **(Matthew 23:27)**. This is the perfect image for the hypocritical husband: polished on the outside, but hollow and decaying on the inside. His home is a graveyard of promises, affection, and intimacy—buried under the weight of duplicity.

The wife of a hypocrite suffers a unique torment. She carries the burden of knowing the truth about the man others admire. She watches him be celebrated while feeling invisible, neglected, or mistreated. She often suffers in silence, because speaking out might bring shame or disbelief. Who would believe her? He's such a "good man." He prays so well. He's always serving. But the hypocrisy robs her of safety. It breeds resentment. It makes her feel like she is part of a spiritual charade.

What makes the hypocrite so destructive is his **double standard**. He expects grace but refuses to give it. He holds his wife to standards he does not keep himself. He may demand respect while speaking to her with contempt. He may insist on spiritual submission while failing to lead in prayer, humility, or love. He is quick to rebuke her flaws but slow to admit his own. This creates an atmosphere of judgment without mercy—a marriage where the wife constantly feels like she's on trial.

Hypocrisy also sabotages the spiritual life of the home. The hypocrite may insist on religious rituals—church attendance, fasting, or family devotions—but these are lifeless routines. The family does not feel drawn to God through him; they feel controlled by religiosity. The children grow cynical. The wife grows weary. 2 Timothy 3:5 describes such people as "having a form of godliness, but denying its power." The hypocrite's home is full of form—but lacks real faith, joy, or power.

Another layer of the hypocrite's danger is **secrecy**. Many live dual lives, not only emotionally but morally. They hide pornography, secret friendships, flirtatious messages, or compromised finances. They justify these by convincing themselves that their public service to God excuses their private sins. But **Galatians 6:7** warns, *"Do not be deceived; God is not mocked: for whatever a man sows, that he will also reap."* Sooner or later, the mask slips. The cracks show. And the fallout is devastating.

The hypocrite often blames his wife for the emotional distance in the marriage. He may say she is "too critical," "not supportive," or "not spiritual enough." But her disconnection is not rooted in rebellion—it is a reaction to his inconsistency. She cannot trust a man who says one thing and lives another. Trust is not built on giftedness—it is built on consistency. And the hypocrite is consistently inconsistent.

Children raised under the leadership of a hypocrite are particularly vulnerable. They learn early that performance matters more than truth. They see their father worship publicly while ignoring, dismissing, or mistreating their mother privately. This creates confusion. Boys may grow up believing that Christianity is about appearance, not transformation. Girls may learn to fear marriage, believing that all men are two-faced. Jesus issued a sobering warning in **Matthew 18:6**: *"Whoever causes one of these little ones to stumble, it would be better for him if a millstone were hung around his neck."* The cost of hypocrisy is generational.

So what does repentance look like for the hypocrite? It begins with **truth-telling**. No more image management. No more double talk. No more spiritual hiding. He must confess—not just his actions, but his attitude. **Psalm 51:6** says, *"Behold, You desire truth in the inward parts."* God wants more than a confession—He demands a transformation of heart.

True repentance also requires **accountability.** The hypocrite must come under spiritual covering, submit to discipleship, and relinquish control. He cannot self-regulate change. He must be challenged. **Hebrews 4:13** declares, *"All things are naked and open to the eyes of Him with whom we have to do."* What he has hidden must be brought into the light. Healing cannot happen in the shadows.

The hypocrite must also **rebuild trust through integrity**, not image. He needs to shift his focus from how others perceive him to how his family experiences him. This means a consistent prayer life, emotional availability, humble apologies, and measurable change. No more sermons without servanthood. No more quoting Scripture while ignoring the Spirit. No more demanding submission while failing to love.

To the wife of a hypocrite: You are not crazy. You are not bitter for seeing what others don't. Your desire for authenticity is righteous. You don't hate God—you hate the lie that has been used in His name. Do not allow yourself to be gaslighted into silence. Seek counsel. Speak the truth. Set boundaries. Your spiritual sanity is worth protecting.

To the church: Stop exalting giftedness over godliness. Stop giving platforms to men who perform well publicly but fail privately. Jesus said in **Matthew 7:16**, *"You shall know them by their fruits."* Not their charisma. Not their following. Not their theological vocabulary. Their fruit. Look at their homes. Look at their marriages. Look at the people closest to them. That is the true measure of leadership.

To the man reading this who sees himself in these words: There is grace, but not without truth. God is not asking for your performance—He wants your repentance. He doesn't want your platform—He wants your posture. **Micah 6:8** says, *"What does the Lord require of you, but to do justly, to love mercy, and to walk humbly with your God?"* Humble yourself. Tell the truth. Start again.

A hypocrite can become a holy man—but only if he chooses honesty over image, humility over ego, and surrender over secrecy. The road to redemption begins where the mask comes off.

Chapter 13

The Dream Killer, Crushing Her Potential

There is a particular kind of man whose impact on his wife is not immediately visible through bruises or screaming matches. His damage is subtler but just as destructive. He doesn't shout her down—he quietly shuts her down. He doesn't physically restrain her, but he emotionally cages her. He is not the angry man, the cheater, or the addict. He is the man who consistently, quietly, and systematically kills his wife's dreams. He is the dream killer—a dangerous man who cannot stand to see the woman beside him rise into the fullness of her God-given purpose.

At the heart of this man is insecurity. Instead of celebrating his wife's gifts, ideas, and callings, he resents them. Her progress feels like a threat. Her passion feels like rebellion. Her ambition becomes an enemy to his ego. Rather than seeing her as a partner in purpose, he views her as a competitor or someone who should remain in his shadow. The dream killer doesn't just dislike her vision—he dismantles it. He calls her dreams unrealistic, her goals prideful, her passions misplaced. Slowly, painfully, she begins to doubt herself.

God did not design marriage to be a place where dreams go to die. He intended it to be a partnership of purpose. In **Genesis 2:18**, the Lord said, *"It is not good that the man should be alone; I will make him a* *helper suitable for him."* The Hebrew phrase "help meet" (*ezer kenegdo*) implies strength corresponding to strength—a suitable counterpart, not a servant. It suggests a woman equipped to aid, challenge, and contribute to a shared vision. When God gave Eve to Adam, He didn't provide a passive bystander. He gave him a powerful partner.

The dream killer twists this divine order. Instead of honoring his wife as a joint heir of purpose (1 Peter 3:7), he diminishes her. He mocks her creativity, restricts her opportunities, and calls her calling a distraction. He labels her fire as rebellion. In doing so, he not only dishonors her but also dishonors the God who placed those gifts within her. **Ephesians 2:10** declares, *"For we are His workmanship, created in Christ Jesus for good works."* The woman is not created to merely serve her husband's dreams—she is created for divine assignments of her own. To suppress her is to sabotage heaven's design.

Often, the dream killer cloaks himself in the garments of tradition. He may use religious language or cultural norms to keep his wife "in her place." He might say, "A woman's place is in the home," or "You're neglecting your family," even when she manages both well. But God never calls a woman to bury her talents in the name of marriage. In Matthew 25, Jesus rebukes the servant who buried his talent out of fear, calling him wicked and lazy. Similarly, many women have buried their gifts in the backyard of their marriage because their husbands couldn't handle their growth.

The **Proverbs 31** woman stands as a striking rebuke to the dream killer. She is entrepreneurial *("She considereth a field, and buyeth it"*—**v.16**), creative *("She maketh herself coverings of tapestry"*—**v.22**), industrious (*"She perceiveth that her merchandise is good"*—**v.18**), and philanthropic (*"She stretcheth out her hand to the poor"*—**v.20**). And what is her husband's response? **Verse 28** says, *"Her husband also, and he praiseth her."* He doesn't compete with her—he celebrates her. He doesn't silence her voice—he honors it. The husband of a virtuous woman becomes her loudest cheerleader, not her greatest hindrance.

The woman married to a dream killer experiences a profound grief. She feels torn between her loyalty to her marriage and the ache in her soul to become what God has called her to be. Every time she shares an idea, she meets resistance. When she tries to step out, she's accused of pride or rebellion. She begins to question whether her passions are even valid. The dream killer doesn't need to scream—he only needs to subtly resist long enough to make her give up.

In some cases, the dream killer becomes **verbally abusive**, using sarcasm, belittlement, or spiritual manipulation. He may quote Scriptures about submission while ignoring verses about mutual honor and sacrifice. **Ephesians 5:25** commands, *"Husbands, love your wives, as Christ also loved the church and gave Himself for it."* Jesus didn't crush the church's potential—He died to awaken it. He didn't compete with her identity—He elevated it.

Some dream-killing husbands hide behind financial control. They refuse to fund their wives' business ideas, educational goals, or ministry endeavors—not because resources are lacking, but because they fear her independence. They weaponize provision. But biblical provision is not for control—it's for empowerment. 1 Timothy 5:8 states that a man who fails to provide is worse than an unbeliever. Provision includes more than food and shelter—it encompasses support for the vision and voice of the woman in his care.

The children in a dream-killed home also suffer. They witness the slow erosion of their mother's identity. Sons learn that women are to be suppressed. Daughters learn that marriage means diminishing oneself. This perpetuates a cycle of passivity and pain across generations. But God's will is for families to be wombs of potential, not prisons of limitation.

So what must a dream-killing man do to change? First, he must **repent of his insecurity**. At its root, his behavior reflects his own lack of identity. A secure man is not intimidated by a strong woman. A godly husband understands that her success is not a threat—it's a testimony. Her elevation does not mean his demotion. As **Ecclesiastes 4:9** says, *"Two are better than one, because they have a good reward for their labor."* Their dreams are meant to multiply, not cancel each other out.

Second, he must **release control**. He must stop trying to dictate her every move and allow her to steward the gifts God placed within her. **Romans 11:29** says, *"For the gifts and calling of God are without repentance."* That means God doesn't take back what He's given her just because her husband disapproves. To fight her calling is to fight God's will. The wise man surrenders his need for dominance and embraces the beauty of co-leadership.

Third, he must **actively support her vision**. This means listening, investing, and advocating. If she wants to write, encourage her. If she wants to launch a business, help her plan. If she wants to go back to school, make space for her. Support is not passive. It's proactive. **Proverbs 18:22** says, *"Whoso findeth a wife findeth a good thing, and obtaineth favour of the Lord."* A woman's dreams are often the doorway to favor for her house.

To the woman whose dreams have been crushed: Take heart. God has not forgotten what He placed inside you. The opposition of man cannot cancel the ordination of God. Your husband may not understand your fire, but heaven does. You were not made to shrink—you were made to shine. Your voice matters. Your vision matters. Your dreams are divine. No man, not even a spouse, has the authority to bury what God has planted.

To pastors and counselors: Teach couples the theology of shared purpose. Equip men to cover without controlling, to lead without limiting. Challenge patriarchal thinking that views a woman's advancement as rebellion. Help families create environments where all gifts—male and female—can flourish.

To the dream killer: If you're reading this, you have a chance to change. Look at your wife again. See the fire that once lit her eyes. Remember the passion she once carried. Ask yourself: Did you celebrate her or suffocate her? It's not too late. Apologize. Repent. Build a new legacy. You don't have to be the man who silenced a prophetess, shut down a Deborah, or discouraged an Esther. You can be the man who unleashed purpose.

Marriage is not a cemetery for dreams. It is the soil where they should grow together. If two walk in agreement, if two dream with unity, if two build with mutual honor—then anything is possible.

Let the dream live again.

Chapter 14

The Dangerous Dudes in the Bible

The Bible reveals not only God's glory but man's brokenness. Scripture is transparent about the failures of men—even those chosen and called by God. These failures, often deeply personal and relational, became national tragedies or family disasters. This chapter explores ten of the most dangerous men in the Bible—men whose decisions devastated their wives, families, and legacies. These are not ancient fairy tales. They are cautionary tales for today's husbands, leaders, and fathers.

1. Adam — The Silent Bystander (Genesis 3)

Adam's greatest failure was not eating the fruit—it was his silence. He stood next to Eve as she was deceived and did nothing. His inaction was the first example of passive male leadership, a pattern that continues to plague marriages today. A man who is physically present but spiritually absent creates an atmosphere where the enemy can easily gain influence.

That moment in the Garden was Adam's opportunity to lead. He could have spoken truth, defended his wife, and challenged the lie. Instead, he blended into the background and allowed deception to reign. Many husbands today say, "It's her life, I don't want to interfere," but spiritual negligence is not neutrality—it is complicity.

Eve's failure may have been one of deception, but Adam's was one of dereliction. His failure to lead, guard, and speak shaped the future of humanity. Men must learn that silence in spiritual matters is never harmless. A husband is called to be a priest, prophet, and protector—not a passive spectator in his home.

2. Abraham — The Fearful Compromiser (Genesis 12 & 20)

Twice, Abraham exposed Sarah to danger by lying to protect himself. His actions were rooted in fear, not faith—ironically, for the man hailed as the "father of faith." When self-preservation becomes stronger than the instinct to protect your wife, you have become dangerous.

Abraham's decisions show how men can spiritualize cowardice. He justified his lie with technicalities ("She is my sister…"), but God did not excuse it. Instead, He intervened directly to protect Sarah, rebuking both Pharaoh and Abimelech. A man who refuses to own his responsibilities often forces God to intervene in ways that reveal his weakness.

Yet, Abraham's story also shows hope. He grew. Later in life, he believed God when told to sacrifice Isaac. This transformation reveals a powerful truth: a man who once endangered his wife can become a man who obeys God radically. But it begins with confronting the fear that makes him selfish.

3. Lot — The Immoral Decision Maker (Genesis 19)

Lot's choice to offer his daughters to an angry mob remains one of the most disturbing acts of paternal failure in Scripture. This action reveals a man so spiritually confused that he would sacrifice his children to protect guests. He had become deeply shaped by the immoral culture of Sodom.

This wasn't a momentary lapse—it was the culmination of years of compromise. Lot had chosen to live near Sodom (Genesis 13:12), then in Sodom, and finally, Sodom lived in him. He failed to discern that his proximity to wickedness had dulled his moral compass. His daughters weren't safe—not from the city, and tragically, not from him.

The incestuous relationship that followed in the mountains (Genesis 19:30–38) wasn't merely a tragedy—it was generational trauma. The Moabites and Ammonites, born from that act, became enemies of Israel. When men compromise their moral convictions, the consequences ripple through generations.

4. Samson — The Unrestrained Lover (Judges 13–16)

Samson had a supernatural calling from birth. As a Nazarite, he was set apart for divine purpose, yet he repeatedly aligned himself with women outside his covenant. He disregarded counsel, ignored warning signs, and allowed lust to govern his decisions.

Delilah was not his first misstep. He had already married a Philistine woman (Judges 14) and slept with a prostitute in Gaza (Judges 16:1). His pattern of behavior reveals a man governed by impulse. Instead of protecting his anointing, he played games with it. His strength made him reckless, not responsible.

Samson's death was a final act of redemption, but it came at the cost of his eyes, freedom, and influence. He died destroying the enemy, but he also died alone. Passion without purpose always leads to destruction. The lesson is clear: a man who won't govern his desires will sabotage his destiny.

5. David — The Abusive King (2 Samuel 11–12)

David's sin with Bathsheba was not simply adultery—it was an abuse of power. As king, his command could not be refused. Bathsheba had no real choice. After impregnating her, David orchestrated Uriah's murder. This was not a moment of weakness; it was a premeditated cover-up by a man who had lost sight of justice.

Nathan's rebuke in **2 Samuel 12** cut deep: "You are the man." David wept and repented, and God forgave—but the sword never departed from his house (2 Samuel 12:10). His son raped his daughter. His family fractured. His leadership credibility suffered. Even forgiven sin has real-world consequences.

Yet David's repentance sets him apart. **Psalm 51** reveals a man broken, not defiant. *"Create in me a clean heart, O God,"* he prayed. Though he failed as a man, he did not harden his heart. Redemption is always possible—but only through deep, humble, contrite repentance.

6. Ahab — The Weak Enabler (1 Kings 21)

Ahab's reign was marked not by tyrannical strength, but by weak compliance. His wife Jezebel committed vile acts in his name, including the murder of Naboth. He allowed evil to rule his house—not because he was inherently evil, but because he lacked the courage to stand firm.

Ahab represents the man who lets his wife manipulate through emotional coercion, vengeance, or spiritual rebellion. He remains passive until provoked and absent until it's too late. His marriage to Jezebel produced a toxic union where she led the house spiritually—and demonic forces were empowered.

God judged Ahab not merely for his actions, but for what he tolerated. In marriage, failing to confront sin is itself sin. Ahab had the position but lacked the presence. The world doesn't need more Ahabs—it needs men who stand in truth, confront injustice, and lead in righteousness.

7. Solomon — The Woman-Worshiper (1 Kings 11)

Solomon began with divine wisdom but ended in bondage. The wisest man on earth made a devastating mistake—he gave his heart to women who did not know his God. His heart turned, not overnight, but gradually, as love and lust replaced loyalty to God.

This was not merely a romantic failure—it was spiritual apostasy. The Bible says, "His wives turned his heart after other gods" (1 Kings 11:4). He built temples for false gods and burned incense to idols. The very man who built the temple of the Lord constructed altars to Molech and Chemosh.

Solomon's life teaches that even the greatest wisdom can be undone by disobedience. When a man's sexual desires override his spiritual walk, destruction is inevitable. God tore the kingdom from his descendants because of this idolatry. No legacy is safe when lust rules the heart.

8. Nabal — The Foolish Husband (1 Samuel 25)

Nabal's foolishness wasn't intellectual—it was emotional and spiritual. He was "harsh and evil in his dealings" (1 Samuel 25:3, NKJV). His wealth fueled his arrogance, and his pride blinded him to danger. When David's men requested food, Nabal insulted them, inviting conflict.

His wife Abigail became the voice of wisdom in their home. Her humility, discernment, and diplomacy saved their household. But imagine the weight she carried—married to a man who brought danger to her door. Nabal was not just foolish; he was reckless and entitled.

God struck him down ten days later. Nabal's story reminds us that foolishness is fatal. A man who rejects wisdom, mocks honor, and disrespects others will eventually fall—either by the hands of men or the judgment of God.

9. Ananias — The Lying Partner (Acts 5:1–10)

Ananias and Sapphira conspired to lie to the apostles about their financial gift. But Ananias initiated the plan. His deception wasn't just toward men—it was against the Holy Spirit (Acts 5:3). The sin was not in the amount given, but in the attempt to appear more generous than they were.

This story is a stern warning against spiritual pretense. Ananias sought the praise of sacrifice without the cost of honesty. He led his wife into a lie, and both died for it. When men fake holiness, they put their homes in spiritual danger.

God's swift judgment wasn't about money—it was about purity in leadership. The early church could not be built on deceit. Ananias teaches us that what a man hides can destroy him—and those he leads.

10. Herod — The People-Pleaser (Mark 6:17–28)

Herod was fascinated by John the Baptist and even feared him, yet he lacked the courage to stand by his convictions. After Herodias's daughter danced for him, Herod made a foolish promise and fulfilled it—beheading a prophet to avoid looking weak.

His moral cowardice cost a righteous man his life. Herod's desire for image management outweighed his fear of God. This is the man who bends to pressure, avoids confrontation, and sells his soul to please the crowd.

Herod's story is a mirror for modern leaders—husbands who sacrifice truth, children who follow trends, and pastors who fear men more than God. When appearance becomes more important than integrity, death follows—sometimes literal, sometimes spiritual.

The Call to Righteous Manhood

These biblical men are not fictional villains—they were real, chosen, and often began their journeys with strength. But at some point, they lost their fear of God, misused their roles, and brought destruction to their families and wives. Some repented and found mercy (like David). Others died in disgrace (like Ananias or Nabal). The thread that binds them all is this: when men fail to lead in righteousness, those closest to them suffer first.

Every man must choose: Will I be a partner in purpose or a perpetrator of pain? Will I build or destroy? Will I be known for character or control?

God is still in the business of redeeming men. He can turn Adams into advocates, Abrahams into protectors, and Solomons into worshipers again. But the first step is confession. The second is submission. The third is daily surrender to the Spirit of God.

As you reflect on these dangerous men of Scripture, ask yourself: Where do I see myself? And more importantly—where do I need to change?

Chapter 15

When Women Break

In every broken marriage where a "dangerous dude" reigns, there is often a broken woman in the shadows—wounded, silenced, discouraged, or emotionally worn. This chapter is not an attack on men, but an honest reflection on the emotional, psychological, spiritual, and physical toll many women suffer in the wake of male irresponsibility and abuse. The wounds left by a narcissist, a controller, a deceiver, or a cheater are not always visible—but they are real, and they run deep.

The Unseen Fracture

When a woman breaks, it doesn't always look like screaming or running. Sometimes it looks like silence. It looks like performing her daily duties, smiling for the children, posting happy photos—but dying inside. She may still cook, clean, serve in church, and uphold her husband's image in public, but her inner self is shattered. Her sense of safety is compromised. Her emotional security is depleted.

Proverbs 14:1 says, *"The wise woman builds her house, but with her own hands the foolish one tears it down."* But what happens when a woman who builds is married to a man who breaks? Her efforts become a matter of survival, not flourishing. She becomes a fixer, a counselor, a lawyer, a nurse, a life coach—everything but a wife at peace. She becomes emotionally overburdened and spiritually disoriented.

Many women suffer in silence because they believe their suffering is godly. They misapply Scripture, enduring abuse as if it's their cross to bear. But while submission is biblical, abuse is not. **Ephesians 5:25** commands, *"Husbands, love your wives, just as Christ loved the church and gave Himself up for her."* Any version of "love" that depletes, demeans, or destroys a woman is not Christlike—it is demonic.

Emotional Abuse: The Invisible Chains

Emotional abuse is often harder to identify than physical abuse, but its effects are just as devastating. Women who suffer emotional abuse endure manipulation, gaslighting, public embarrassment, chronic criticism, and controlling behavior. They are made to feel crazy, inadequate, or guilty for things they didn't do. Their self-esteem erodes day by day.

The Weapon of Words

The words of a husband should be safe. **Proverbs 18:21** reminds us, *"Death and life are in the power of the tongue."* But in many homes, words have become weapons. Sarcasm, comparison, shouting, passive aggression, and intentional silence are used to destabilize and dominate. The woman begins to walk on eggshells. She questions her worth. She may even believe she deserves the treatment she's receiving.

God never intended marriage to be a prison. It is a covenant of mutual honor. **1 Peter 3:7** commands husbands to dwell with their wives *"according to knowledge, giving honor to the wife, as to the weaker vessel... that your prayers be not hindered."* A dishonorable man not only hurts his wife—he hinders his connection with God. When women break under emotional abuse, heaven mourns.

Sexual Neglect and Abuse

The marriage bed is meant to be a place of safety, pleasure, and intimacy—not fear or rejection. Yet many women suffer quietly in their bedrooms. Some are sexually starved—ignored, withheld from, or treated as an afterthought. Others are sexually abused—coerced, violated, or treated like property. These experiences break a woman's soul.

In 1 Corinthians 7:3–4, Paul teaches that in marriage, both husband and wife owe each other "conjugal rights." The body of one belongs to the other. But this is not a license for domination—it's a call to mutual consent and care. Sexual intimacy is not about performance but about covenantal connection. When that sacred space becomes abusive or cold, it sends a woman into emotional exile.

Broken women in these conditions often lose their sense of desirability. They may internalize rejection as personal failure. They may grow resentful, bitter, or numb. The body God gave them becomes a battlefield—where shame, silence, and confusion replace joy and union. No woman should endure sexual trauma in a place God designed for sacred delight.

Spiritual Suppression

Some men use Scripture as a weapon—twisting biblical roles to silence, subjugate, or disqualify their wives from purpose. These "religious abusers" control with chapter and verse, demanding submission while rejecting accountability. They mock their wives' dreams. They prevent them from speaking in church, studying, preaching, leading, or growing. These women are not just breaking emotionally—they are breaking spiritually.

This is not biblical order; it is spiritual suppression. Jesus welcomed, affirmed, and elevated women. He revealed Himself first to a woman after His resurrection (John 20:14–18). He allowed a sinful woman to anoint Him (Luke 7:37–38). He taught women (Luke 10:39). He protected women from public shame (John 8:11). Any form of Christianity that silences, shames, or sidelines a woman is not the way of Christ.

A broken woman in this space feels far from God—even when she's in church every Sunday. She doubts her calling. She stops dreaming. She may even believe her purpose died the day she said, "I do." But God sees her. Like Hagar in the wilderness, God finds her and says, *"You are the God who sees me"* **(Genesis 16:13).** Even when her husband doesn't, God does.

When Women Snap: The Dangerous Response

Not every broken woman stays silent. Some eventually snap. Their pain becomes rage. Their despair turns into destruction. They may cheat, abandon the home, curse God, or descend into addictions. Though these actions are not justified, they are often rooted in years of unaddressed trauma.

This is the woman who has given all she had. She begged for counseling. She tried submission. She turned the other cheek. But one day, she stopped crying and started planning her escape. Her "rebellion" is often a reaction to a decade of denial. Her meltdown is a mirror of the mistreatment she endured.

Proverbs 21:9 says, *"Better to live on a corner of the roof than share a house with a quarrelsome wife."* Many men quote this verse but fail to ask what turned her into that woman. Sometimes, behind a quarrelsome wife is a negligent, controlling, or abusive husband. When a woman breaks, she either withers or fights to survive.

Children of Broken Women

The pain of a broken woman rarely ends with her. Children watch their mother suffer in silence. They internalize fear, dysfunction, and conflict. Daughters may inherit low self-worth. Sons may become emotionally distant or replicate their father's patterns. The atmosphere of a home where a woman is breaking becomes toxic to the next generation.

Titus 2:4 calls older women to *"teach the young women to love their husbands and children."* But how can a woman teach love if she's never received it? How can she model wholeness while bleeding on the inside? Broken women often raise broken children—not because they lack love, but because they lack protection.

The generational impact of a dangerous man is measured not just in his marriage, but in his lineage. A woman's breaking is not just her pain—it is the breaking of a culture, a legacy, a future. The healing of the woman is the healing of the home.

The Role of the Church

The church must become a refuge for broken women—not a trap. Too often, women are told to "go back and pray harder" without real investigation. Pastors may side with abusers. Counseling can be one-sided. The appearance of a happy marriage is often prioritized over the health of the individuals in it.

James 1:27 says, *"Religion that God our Father accepts... is this: to look after orphans and widows in their distress..."* We must expand this care to include the emotionally widowed—those whose husbands are present in body but absent in heart. The church must protect, advocate, and intervene when needed.

Jesus, the Defender of the Broken

Jesus is the defender of the broken. He declared in **Luke 4:18**, *"He has sent Me to bind up the brokenhearted..."* The church must echo this mission. It must make room for women's voices, offer safe counseling, confront abusive leaders, and teach healthy manhood and womanhood with equal weight.

Restoration for the Broken Woman

God doesn't just pity broken women—He restores them. In **Joel 2:25**, He promises, *"I will restore to you the years that the locusts have eaten."* No matter how deep the trauma or how long the suffering, God can rebuild what was lost. The key is surrender, safety, and truth.

Some women will experience restoration within their marriage—if the man repents and changes. Others may find healing after separation or divorce. In both cases, healing requires truth-telling, therapy, prayer, community, and a deep reintroduction to their identity in Christ.

Psalm 147:3 says, *"He heals the brokenhearted and binds up their wounds."* God does not discard the broken woman—He gathers her. He does not shame her story—He redeems it. She is still worthy, still loved, still called, still whole in Him.

Conclusion: A Call to Healing

When women break, the world loses light. The enemy knows this, which is why he targets marriages through the negligence and sins of dangerous men. But healing is possible. Women can rise again. They can sing again. They can trust again. And yes—they can love again.

To the broken woman reading this: You are not crazy. You are not weak. You are not alone. God sees your pain. He knows your tears. And He is not silent. Your healing begins with truth. The truth is—what broke you is not your fault, and it is not the end of your story.

Let this chapter be a line in the sand. No more breaking in silence. No more enduring without help. No more bleeding behind closed doors. Jesus came to bind up the brokenhearted—and that includes **you.**

Chapter 16

The Journey to Healing, Rebuilding After the Ruin

The journey from devastation to healing is not easy, but it is possible. Many women—and some men—who have endured the fallout of being in a relationship with a "dangerous dude" feel like their lives are beyond repair. They carry wounds not just on the surface, but in the deepest parts of their soul. Some feel they've wasted years, lost themselves, or died slowly inside. But this chapter is a roadmap for recovery. It is a compassionate yet truthful invitation to begin again not just with survival, but with restoration, wholeness, and joy.

The Shattered Self — When Identity Is Lost

When a person lives under prolonged emotional, spiritual, or physical abuse, the first casualty is their sense of identity. Victims of manipulation, control, gaslighting, and neglect often become hollow versions of their former selves. The woman who once laughed freely, danced, and dreamed becomes afraid of her own voice. The man who once loved deeply begins to shut down emotionally just to cope. Identity is assaulted first.

In **Genesis 1:27**, the Bible says, *"So God created man in His own image... male and female He created them."* Our sense of self—our confidence, voice, and personhood—is tied to the image of God. When someone repeatedly violates that image through dishonor, we begin to doubt who we are. We start believing the lies spoken over us: "You're too much. You're too sensitive. You're not enough."

Healing begins when we return to the truth of who we are. **Psalm 139:14** declares, *"I am fearfully and wonderfully made."* Even if a spouse didn't affirm your worth, God already has. His voice must override every voice that ever tore you down. Recovery starts by letting the Creator restore His image in you.

Breaking the Soul Tie — Reclaiming the Mind and Emotions

A soul tie is more than an emotional connection—it is a spiritual entanglement. When a person has poured years of love, sacrifice, sex, support, and devotion into someone—even someone who misused them—it creates a bond that doesn't easily break. That's why many people stay long after a relationship turns toxic. Their soul is tied, not just their heart.

Breaking the Soul Tie — Reclaiming the Mind and Emotions

In **1 Corinthians 6:16**, Paul asks, *"Do you not know that he who unites himself with a prostitute is one with her in body?"* He wasn't merely talking about sex. He was addressing fusion—the spiritual merging that occurs in intimacy, whether healthy or unhealthy. This is why some women remain attached to a man who cheated, abused, or abandoned them. Their soul still echoes a connection that must be severed.

Breaking a soul tie requires intentional steps: confession, prayer, counseling, fasting, boundaries, and often a radical emotional detox. **Isaiah 58:6** says, *"Is not this the kind of fasting I have chosen: to loose the chains of injustice and untie the cords of the yoke?"* There is a fast that unties you from the one who bound you.

Confronting the Pain — Owning the Story

Healing doesn't come by ignoring pain; it comes by confronting it. Many survivors try to skip this step. They rush into new relationships, drown themselves in church work, or pretend to be okay. But the soul doesn't heal through avoidance—it heals through truth.

In John 4, Jesus met a woman at the well who had five husbands and was living with a sixth man. She was broken, shamed, and used to being dismissed. But Jesus confronted her story. He said, *"You have had five husbands"* **(John 4:18)**—not to shame her, but to set her free. He saw her pain. He named it. And then He offered her living water.

Your healing starts when you stop hiding your story. You don't have to announce it to everyone, but you do need to tell it to God, a counselor, a trusted mentor, or even journal it for yourself. Naming your pain is not weakness—it is warfare.

Forgiveness — Letting Go of the Poison

Forgiveness is one of the most challenging parts of the healing journey, especially when the offender shows no remorse. Some dangerous men walk away unrepentant, proud, or quickly remarrying—leaving their victims crushed and enraged. The injustice is real. But the choice to forgive is not about them—it's about you.

Ephesians 4:31–32 urges, *"Let all bitterness, wrath, and anger... be put away from you... Be kind to one another, tenderhearted, forgiving one another, as God in Christ forgave you."* Forgiveness doesn't excuse the abuse or require reconciliation. It means choosing not to carry the cancer of offense.

Unforgiveness binds you to the offender emotionally. It's a spiritual tether that keeps you locked in the past. Letting go isn't forgetting—it's cutting the cord that chokes your joy. It's saying, "I release you from my courtroom and place you in God's hands."

Reclaiming Your Voice — Speaking After Silence

Many broken people lose their voice in trauma. They stop speaking up, dreaming aloud, or expressing opinions and emotions. They believe their voice caused problems, so they choose silence. But God is restoring the voice of the broken.

Jeremiah 1:9 says, *"Then the Lord reached out His hand and touched my mouth and said to me, 'I have put My words in your mouth.'"* Even if man tried to mute you, God has something to say through you. Your testimony matters. Your perspective matters. Your feelings matter.

One powerful step in healing is reclaiming your narrative. Write your story. Speak in safe spaces. Share your testimony. Declare affirmations over yourself daily. Create new declarations of life. Let the enemy know—your voice has returned.

Rebuilding Boundaries — Guarding the Garden

After trauma, the soul is like a garden that's been trampled. The soil may still be fertile, but fences must be built before new seeds are planted. Boundaries are not walls to keep people out—they're gates to control what comes in.

Proverbs 4:23 says, *"Above all else, guard your heart, for everything you do flows from it."* Healing includes saying "no" without guilt, setting emotional limits, cutting off toxic access, and choosing peace over people-pleasing. It means no longer sacrificing your sanity for someone else's approval.

Rebuilding your life requires healthy parameters: spiritual, emotional, relational, and physical. This includes choosing which conversations to entertain, which environments to re-enter, and how much access others have to your time and energy.

Reconnecting with God — The Ultimate Healer

Some people are wounded not only by men but also in their faith. When the dangerous dude was a pastor, a worship leader, or a man who claimed to love God, the confusion runs deep. Victims begin to associate God with abuse. They pull away from prayer. Worship feels dry. Scripture feels empty.

But God is not like man. He is the faithful Husband (Isaiah 54:5). He is gentle and lowly (Matthew 11:29). He is near to the brokenhearted

(Psalm 34:18). He weeps with you. He covers you. He never violated or manipulated you. And He longs to restore your trust.

The healing journey must bring you back to His feet—not in performance, but in presence. Sit with Him again. Cry before Him. Tell Him the whole truth. You'll find that His silence is not neglect—it's comfort. His Word will become balm. His Spirit will become oil. You are safe with Him.

Rebirthing Purpose — Beauty from Ashes

The final stage of healing is rediscovering purpose. **Isaiah 61:3** promises that God will give you *"beauty for ashes, the oil of joy for mourning, and a garment of praise for a spirit of despair."* Your pain can birth purpose. Your ashes can birth anointing.

Some of the most powerful ministries, books, businesses, and healing movements are born from pain. The woman who was once silenced becomes a coach for others. The man who endured emotional trauma becomes a voice for healthy masculinity. The survivor becomes the speaker, the mentor, the author.

Don't rush this stage. Let God write it. But know—your pain will not be wasted. He bottles every tear (Psalm 56:8). He records every cry. And when the time comes, He will put your testimony on display—not for your glory, but for the healing of many.

Conclusion: From Ruins to Redemption

This book began with a warning—to identify dangerous men. But it ends with a promise: God can heal the brokenhearted. Whether you've been hurt by betrayal, neglect, abuse, or abandonment, your story is not over. You are not disqualified. You are not too damaged. And you are not alone.

The journey to healing is not a sprint—it's a sacred walk with the Holy Spirit. One layer at a time. One tear at a time. One truth at a time. You are allowed to grieve. You are allowed to feel. But more importantly, you are allowed to heal.

From the ashes of devastation will rise a healed version of you—not bitter, but wiser; not hardened, but whole; not silent, but strong. You will rebuild. You will rejoice. And you will never settle again for anything less than what God designed you to receive.

Because you are worthy. You are chosen. And most of all—you are being made new.

CHAPTER 17

The Religious Manipulator, Misusing God to Control Her

There is perhaps no more insidious form of abuse than spiritual manipulation, especially when cloaked in the language of God. The religious manipulator is a husband who twists Scripture, distorts theology, and weaponizes faith to control, silence, and dominate his wife. On the outside, he may appear devout—attending church regularly, quoting Bible verses, and insisting he is the "head of the house." But behind closed doors, his spiritual authority becomes a straitjacket that restricts, rather than empowers, his spouse.

This chapter is an urgent call to unmask the misuse of Scripture in the home and expose the dangerous effects of religious abuse in marriage. It is not an attack on headship or God-ordained roles, but a defense of true Christlike leadership and biblical integrity.

A Distorted Theology of Headship

One of the most commonly misused passages by religious manipulators is Ephesians 5:22: "Wives, submit yourselves to your own husbands, as to the Lord." With this verse, many of these men construct a theology of unchecked dominance, expecting their wives to obey without question. They interpret submission as slavery and authority as entitlement.

Yet they rarely quote the following verses: *"For the husband is the head of the wife, as Christ is the head of the church... and gave Himself for her"* **(Ephesians 5:23–25)**. Christlike headship is not about control; it's about sacrifice. Jesus washed feet. He laid down His life. He empowered others. That is the model of headship Scripture teaches—not domination, but loving leadership rooted in servanthood.

The religious manipulator disregards this balance. His understanding of the Bible is shallow and self-serving. He cherry-picks verses to justify emotional, financial, sexual, or even physical abuse. His version of Scripture is stripped of grace and inflated with ego.

The Idol of Patriarchy

Many men who manipulate their wives religiously have made an idol out of patriarchy. They are less interested in spiritual growth and more obsessed with preserving their position as "king of the castle." Their identity is deeply tied to power, and religion becomes a convenient tool to reinforce it.

This patriarchal idolatry can be subtle. For example, a husband may forbid his wife from working—not out of biblical conviction, but out of insecurity and fear of her independence. He may limit her access to money, spiritual resources, or ministry opportunities—all under the guise of "submission." In these cases, the issue isn't theology—it's control dressed in religious robes.

Micah 6:8 tells us what God truly requires of a man: *"To do justly, to love mercy, and to walk humbly with your God."* There is no humility in manipulation. There is no justice in spiritual suppression. And there is no mercy in using the Bible as a whip instead of a lamp.

Keeping Her in a Religious Cocoon

One of the most tragic effects of religious manipulation is how it traps a wife in a cocoon of fear, guilt, and false teaching. She begins to believe her suffering is godly, her silence is virtuous, and challenging her husband is rebellious. Her spiritual growth is stunted. Her voice is silenced. Her identity is lost.

This religious cocoon becomes a prison. She may fear reading the Bible for herself because he's told her she "can't interpret it right." She may avoid asking questions in church because he says she's "out of order." She may suppress her spiritual gifts, callings, and ideas because he believes God only speaks through him.

This is not biblical. **Galatians 3:28** declares, *"There is neither male nor female, for you are all one in Christ Jesus."* The same Holy Spirit that filled Peter at Pentecost filled Mary, Elizabeth, and Priscilla. A godly husband doesn't fear his wife's anointing—he celebrates it. He doesn't silence her insight—he draws from it. He doesn't keep her small—he calls her higher.

Gaslighting with Scripture

One of the signature behaviors of the religious manipulator is spiritual gaslighting. He twists Scriptures to make his wife doubt her own sanity, memories, and convictions. If she expresses pain, he says she's "being emotional." If she questions his actions, he calls it "rebellion." If she seeks counsel elsewhere, he accuses her of "dishonoring spiritual authority."

This is not only manipulative—it's evil. Jesus had strong words for such behavior. In **Matthew 23:4**, He rebuked the Pharisees, saying, *"They tie up heavy, cumbersome loads and put them on other people's shoulders, but they themselves are not willing to lift a finger to move them."* These religious leaders, like manipulative husbands today, imposed spiritual burdens while refusing to walk in love.

The wife of such a man often lives in confusion. She doubts her discernment. She fears hell for speaking up. She may feel distant from God—not realizing that it's not God who has rejected her, but her husband who has misrepresented Him.

False Authority and the Jezebel Smokescreen

Another tactic of the religious manipulator is labeling his wife as "Jezebel" whenever she challenges his authority or expresses discomfort. The spirit of Jezebel, described in Revelation 2:20, is a real threat in the church—but it is often misused to shut down strong, discerning, and intelligent women.

When a wife raises a valid concern, he accuses her of being controlling. If she asks for mutual submission, he calls her rebellious. This false narrative conveniently keeps him in the driver's seat and her in the backseat of spiritual development.

But **1 Peter 3:7** gives clear instruction: *"Husbands, in the same way, be considerate as you live with your wives, and treat them with respect as the weaker partner and as heirs with you of the gracious gift of life, so that nothing will hinder your prayers."* A man who dishonors his wife—even if he quotes Scripture while doing it—will find his own prayers blocked. God is not impressed by spiritual talk that lacks spiritual fruit.

Unlearning Religion, Rediscovering Jesus

The way out of religious manipulation is not rebellion, but reformation. Many women trapped in religiously abusive marriages must embark on a journey of unlearning distorted religion and rediscovering the heart of Jesus. He is not a taskmaster. He is not a tyrant. He is not an insecure male figure demanding silence. He is the Bridegroom who elevates, honors, and heals His bride.

John 10:10 reminds us of His purpose: *"The thief comes only to steal and kill and destroy; I have come that they may have life, and have it to the full."* Religious manipulation steals life. Jesus restores it. He affirms her voice. He gently corrects, not condemns. He invites dialogue, not dictatorship.

Wives in this situation must reconnect with Scripture for themselves in safe spaces—through study groups, mentorship, and personal prayer. They must discern between the voice of God and the echo of manipulation. The truth will set them free (John 8:32).

The Call to the Church

Religious manipulators often thrive in environments where church culture reinforces silence, male dominance, and the idolization of titles. Sadly, many churches have failed to hold men accountable for their misuse of Scripture in the home. Instead of challenging spiritual abuse, they spiritualize it.

The church must rise with prophetic boldness. Leaders must preach the whole counsel of God, teaching mutual honor, servant leadership, and the fruits of the Spirit. Pastoral counseling must include trauma awareness. Premarital classes must address spiritual abuse. And women must be encouraged to study the Word deeply—not just listen to it.

Titus 2:1–5 outlines how older women are to train younger women, but the church must also raise strong men who understand the difference between biblical leadership and egotistical control. We need husbands like Boaz, not Nabal; leaders like Joseph, not Ahab.

Conclusion: Freedom from the Religious Cage

A husband who uses God to control his wife is not leading—he is violating. God never gave men the authority to override their wives' personhood. He gave them the charge to love as Christ loved. That kind of love doesn't manipulate—it liberates.

To the woman caught in this religious cocoon, hear the voice of Jesus: *"Come to Me, all you who are weary and burdened, and I will give you rest"* **(Matthew 11:28).** Lay down the burden of religious fear. Rise into the light of truth. Rediscover the beauty of God apart from the voice of abuse.

To the man who recognizes himself in these words, repentance is still available. True authority is earned through service, not seized through

Scripture. Return to the feet of Jesus and relearn what it means to lead like Him. There is still time to become the man God intended.

Chapter 18

The Criminal Husband, When Silence Becomes Complicity

Marriage binds two people into a sacred covenant, not only of love and intimacy but of truth and integrity. It is a relationship meant to be built on mutual trust, transparency, and righteousness. But what happens when the man a woman marries is not just difficult or flawed—but criminal? What if he is not only breaking hearts but breaking laws? What if behind closed doors, a man becomes a predator, a thief, or a fraudster, while his wife carries the unbearable weight of knowing—and saying nothing?

This is the dark reality of many marriages: women yoked to men whose actions are not only morally wrong but legally punishable. These husbands steal from their companies, cheat on taxes, defraud the government, abuse children, commit acts of sexual violence—even within their own families—and expect their wives to remain quiet under the guise of "submission," "support," or "loyalty." The wife is caught in a prison of secrecy, guilt, and fear, torn between protecting her husband and protecting the truth.

This chapter is a sobering confrontation with the Criminal Husband—a man who uses marriage not as a platform for covenantal holiness, but as a cloak for corruption. And it is a call for wives in this situation to understand their moral, spiritual, and even legal responsibility—not to cover evil, but to confront it.

The Many Faces of Criminality in Marriage

Criminal husbands come in many forms, and not all wear the face of the stereotypical gangster or felon. Some are church leaders embezzling funds. Others are respected executives falsifying financial records. Some are charming fathers who secretly molest their daughters. Others are men who have raped their own wives under the false assumption that marriage is a license to violate consent.

Here are some sobering categories:

1. **The White-Collar Criminal**

    This man may be involved in tax evasion, company fraud, insider trading, or money laundering. He manipulates systems and finances with a clean face and an expensive suit. His wife may become aware of falsified books, stolen accounts, or shady deals but is told to "stay out of it." The crime is hidden behind success, and the wife becomes an unwilling accomplice.

2. **The Sexual Offender**

    One of the most horrifying realities is the wife who discovers her husband is sexually abusing children—sometimes even their own. Others find their husbands addicted to child pornography or committing sexual assaults against unsuspecting women. The emotional trauma of discovering this is devastating, but what follows is often worse: the pressure to stay silent for the sake of "family," reputation, or fear of retaliation.

3. **The Violent Criminal**

   Some men are involved in gangs, illegal weapons, domestic violence rings, or have a long rap sheet buried under sealed records. These men may act pious in public but are dangerous behind closed doors. Their wives often live in fear—silenced by threats, financial dependency, or the shame of what the community might think.

4. **The Predator in the Pulpit**

   Some criminal husbands are pastors, prophets, or church elders. They use the Bible to hide their criminal acts—from sexual exploitation of minors to financial theft from congregations. The wife may be aware but is often complicit by silence, fear, or a distorted sense of spiritual submission.

Biblical Truth: God Does Not Protect the Wicked

Scripture is clear: *"He who conceals his sins does not prosper, but whoever confesses and renounces them finds mercy"* **(Proverbs 28:13).** Silence in the face of wickedness is not loyalty—it is complicity. Covering up criminal behavior is not righteousness—it is rebellion against God's justice.

Ananias and Sapphira (Acts 5:1–11) offer a sobering lesson. Together, as husband and wife, they conspired to lie to the Holy Spirit about the proceeds of a land sale. Sapphira could have told the truth after Ananias died—but she chose to repeat the lie. Both died on the spot. Their story is not just about dishonesty; it's about spiritual and marital collusion with sin. Sapphira wasn't judged for her husband's actions. She was judged for her agreement with them.

Wives must understand: you will not be judged by God for betraying your criminal husband's secrets—you will be held accountable if you support or conceal them.

When Loyalty Becomes a Lie

There is a toxic teaching in some circles that a wife must protect her husband's reputation at all costs. But biblical submission is not a license for lawlessness. Loyalty to a criminal man is disloyalty to God. Keeping secrets that harm others is not nobility—it is complicity.

Esther is a model of righteous courage. She risked her life to expose Haman's evil plot, even though it threatened her marriage and status. Abigail disobeyed her wicked husband Nabal to save her household and honor God (1 Samuel 25). God honored her disobedience to a fool and elevated her after Nabal died. These women did not protect evil. They protected righteousness.

The Price of Silence: Emotional and Legal Fallout

Remaining silent while your husband commits crimes can have devastating consequences:

1. Legal Consequences

Remaining silent in the face of your husband's criminal activity can expose you to serious legal liability. Many jurisdictions classify this as aiding and abetting, obstruction of justice, or being an accessory after the fact—depending on your level of knowledge and involvement. Even if you did not commit the crime yourself, your failure to report or your participation in covering it up could lead to fines, arrest, or imprisonment. Laws are designed not only to punish perpetrators but also to hold accountable those who enable wrongdoing by their silence.

If you are financially benefiting from your husband's crimes—whether it's stolen money, unreported income, or fraudulently obtained assets—you could be forced to forfeit those gains. Law enforcement may seize your bank accounts, vehicles, or properties during investigations. If you co-signed documents or allowed the use of your name for illegal activities, you may be legally entangled for years. Silence is not just a moral compromise—it is legal entrapment.

In cases involving abuse, especially child sexual abuse or domestic violence, mandatory reporting laws can place the burden squarely on you. Professionals like teachers, counselors, and healthcare workers are legally bound to report abuse, but even as a spouse, you may be held liable if you knew abuse was occurring and chose not to act. Courts take the safety of victims seriously, and they may view your inaction as willful negligence or complicity.

Furthermore, your silence can backfire in divorce or custody proceedings. If the truth eventually emerges—and it often does—you may lose credibility in court. Judges want to see that a parent is acting in the best interest of the child. If you knowingly kept children in a harmful or illegal environment, you may lose custody or visitation rights. The law may interpret your silence not as protection, but as a betrayal of your parental duty.

2. Moral Consequences

The moral toll of living with the knowledge of your husband's crimes is often heavier than the fear of public exposure. A woman who carries a secret of darkness within her marriage eventually becomes a prisoner of her own conscience. Each day, she is forced to suppress her convictions, silence her integrity, and tiptoe around the truth. Over time, this inner tension begins to erode her sense of self-worth, righteousness, and spiritual peace.

There is a slow but real decay that happens to the soul when truth is buried. Silence in the face of evil fosters guilt, shame, and internal conflict. You may begin to feel like a stranger in your own skin, wondering whether God still hears your prayers or if your silence has disqualified you from His mercy. But remember: it is never too late to repent, speak out, and realign yourself with the truth. *"If we confess our sins, he is faithful and just to forgive us our sins and to purify us from all unrighteousness"* **(1 John 1:9)**.

Moral silence doesn't just affect your relationship with yourself and God—it impacts your relationships with others. You may become emotionally distant from friends or family because you're afraid they'll uncover the truth. You might withdraw from church, become defensive in conversations, or overcompensate with artificial smiles. Living a double life creates internal fractures that eventually begin to show externally.

And morally, you're not just responsible for what you do—you're responsible for what you allow. **James 4:17** is blunt: *"Anyone who knows the good they ought to do and doesn't do it, sins."* The longer you justify silence as wisdom, the more you normalize evil. Eventually, your heart becomes numb to the conviction of the Holy Spirit. Don't let silence cost you your moral compass.

3. Spiritual Consequences

The spiritual consequences of remaining silent while your husband engages in criminal activity can be devastating. Silence in the presence of sin separates you from intimacy with God. **Isaiah 59:2** says, *"But your iniquities have separated you from your God; your sins have hidden his face from you, so that he will not hear."* When you protect darkness, you forfeit divine fellowship. The Spirit of God is grieved not only by the acts of the wicked but also by the silence of the righteous.

Your spiritual authority is weakened when you refuse to stand for truth. A wife who remains silent in the face of abuse or corruption often finds that her prayers lose their power, her worship feels hollow, and her joy is choked out by shame. The presence of unconfessed knowledge becomes a spiritual stronghold. Demons feed on secrecy. And what is unexposed remains unhealed. Spiritual warfare cannot be waged effectively when you are silently standing on the wrong side of righteousness.

Moreover, your silence could enable generational curses. By allowing sin to remain in the home unchallenged, you create an atmosphere where future generations may suffer. Children may carry emotional scars, develop warped views of marriage, or repeat the cycle of abuse and criminality. **Exodus 20:5** warns that *"the iniquity of the fathers"* can affect *"the third and fourth generation."* But you have the power to stop that cycle—by exposing the sin, not excusing it.

Finally, understand that God is a God of justice. He doesn't just call us to love mercy—He calls us to "do justly" (Micah 6:8). When you protect criminal behavior in the name of marriage, you stand against the very justice that God loves. But when you choose truth, even at personal cost, heaven stands with you. Your obedience becomes a fragrant offering to the Lord. It's never too late to shift from spiritual compromise to covenant alignment.

Advice to Wives Living This Nightmare

If you are a wife dealing with a criminal husband, here is wisdom to navigate your way forward:

1. Document Everything

If you've discovered your husband is engaging in criminal activity—whether it's embezzlement, abuse, rape, or incest—the first step is to begin documenting what you know. Memories can become cloudy under pressure, especially when trauma and fear are involved. Keeping a detailed written or digital log with dates, descriptions, and any physical evidence (texts, photos, voicemails, financial documents) becomes your safeguard when and if you need to report him to authorities.

Documentation protects your integrity. Should law enforcement become involved, or if custody battles ensue, the truth will not rest on your testimony alone—it will be supported by written, recorded facts. Many women have lost their cases in court because they failed to maintain records. Judges and investigators cannot act solely on emotion; they need documented proof. This is not about vengeance—it is about justice and protection.

Spiritually, keeping records does not make you a traitor. It makes you a steward of truth. **Proverbs 14:25** says, *"A truthful witness saves* *lives, but a false witness is deceitful."* Your record may be the very thing that saves someone else—perhaps even a child—from harm. Don't dismiss the power of your diligence in this area.

2. Seek Godly, Legal Counsel Immediately

The moment you become aware of your husband's criminal conduct, the clock starts ticking. Waiting, praying silently, or "hoping it stops" is not a plan. You need both spiritual and legal counsel from people who will honor your story and help you navigate with wisdom. A godly pastor, a licensed Christian counselor, and a lawyer who handles criminal or domestic cases should be your immediate points of contact.

Legal counsel helps you understand what the law requires of you as someone who knows about a crime. In many jurisdictions, knowing and failing to report certain crimes—especially those involving children—can result in legal consequences. Don't make assumptions. Seek clarity from someone trained to interpret the law. Ignorance will not protect you in a court of law, nor will blind loyalty be a defense before God.

In tandem with legal steps, you must also seek godly counsel. Do not speak to just any church leader. Speak to those trained in trauma, abuse recovery, and spiritual formation. Some pastors may advise you to "stay and pray," but others—those truly rooted in Scripture—will echo Jesus' model of confronting evil and protecting the innocent. Remember: The Holy Spirit is called the Counselor. Let His wisdom guide you through counselors who know both law and truth.

3. Do Not Confront Him Alone

The temptation to confront your husband by yourself may seem courageous, but it can be incredibly dangerous. Criminal men, especially those engaged in high-stakes crimes or deep-seated perversion, may react violently, defensively, or manipulatively. The more serious the crime, the more careful you must be in how you approach disclosure or confrontation.

In many cases, wives have been physically assaulted or psychologically terrorized after challenging their husbands. Others have had their evidence destroyed, their reputation smeared, or been gaslighted into believing they were imagining things. The enemy often operates in secrecy and confusion. Confronting a criminal without support or safety mechanisms opens you up to spiritual and physical retaliation.

Instead, bring light and witnesses into the situation. Whether through a counselor, a church leader, or law enforcement, ensure someone else is present. If the situation is severe, confront through legal channels, not personal confrontation. **Proverbs 11:14** reminds us, *"In the multitude of counselors there is safety."* Safety is not just spiritual—it is strategic. Don't fight alone what should be exposed with help.

4. Protect Children at All Costs

If children are in the home, your first and highest moral responsibility is to shield them from harm, not to maintain the illusion of a functioning marriage. No amount of marital loyalty is worth the trauma of a child being abused, manipulated, or exposed to criminal behavior. You are not betraying your husband by protecting your children—you are fulfilling your God-given duty.

Many women convince themselves that if the abuse hasn't touched the child directly, they can stay silent. But indirect abuse—exposure to violence, threats, fear, or secrecy—is just as damaging. Studies show that children who grow up in homes where criminal or abusive behavior is hidden are more likely to replicate those patterns, become emotionally stunted, or struggle with trust and identity into adulthood.

The Bible is clear on this matter. Jesus said in **Matthew 18:6**, *"But whoever causes one of these little ones who believe in Me to stumble, it would be better for him to have a millstone hung around his neck,* *and to be drowned in the depth of the sea."* There is no compromise here. A man who endangers a child—by action or neglect—has forfeited his authority as a protector. Remove the child. Remove yourself. And rebuild with help.

5. Break the Silence

Evil thrives in darkness, and secrets give it oxygen. One of the most powerful things you can do is speak. Tell someone. Whether it's a close friend, a spiritual mentor, or law enforcement, your silence is not a shield—it's a snare. The longer you remain silent, the more your husband's criminal behavior continues unchecked, potentially hurting others or escalating in severity.

Breaking the silence is not betrayal—it is intercession. When you speak out, you are not just escaping—you are intervening. You become a voice for justice, for the abused, and for righteousness. Remember Esther, who had to break royal protocol to expose Haman's evil. Had she remained silent, an entire nation would have perished. Your voice has the power to shift destinies.

Additionally, the emotional healing that comes from telling your story cannot be overstated. The weight of secrecy is often heavier than the crime itself. The moment you speak, the grip of fear loosens. Healing begins when light enters. **Ephesians 5:11** commands: *"Have nothing to do with the fruitless deeds of darkness, but rather expose them."* Your voice is a weapon. Use it.

6. Pray for Courage and Deliverance

Prayer is not a substitute for action—it is the fuel that sustains it. In a situation involving criminal behavior, fear can be paralyzing. You will need supernatural courage, peace, and clarity to walk through the valley ahead. Cry out to God. He hears. He sees. And He will strengthen you. **Psalm 34:17** says, *"The righteous cry out, and the Lord hears them; He delivers them from all their troubles."*

Pray not only for the strength to leave or confront but also for emotional and mental healing. Pray for the courage to deal with the fallout—family members who may not understand, a church community that may take sides, or a legal process that may be grueling. God does not promise comfort without conflict, but He does promise victory through obedience.

Also pray for your husband—but do not confuse intercession with intimacy. It is okay to be separate from someone and still petition God for their salvation or repentance. Boundaries are biblical. Moses interceded for Pharaoh, but he didn't live in his palace. Pray fiercely, walk wisely, and never forget that the Lord is close to the brokenhearted and saves those who are crushed in spirit (Psalm 34:18).

Final Words to the Wife Caught in the Middle

Dear sister, you did not choose this man's crimes. But now that you know, you must choose righteousness. You are not alone. God does not want you enslaved to a man's darkness. He wants you aligned with His light. Your silence may seem like protection—but it will only shield sin. Your voice may feel like betrayal—but it may be the very thing that sets others free.

The day you speak, heaven will stand with you. Angels will guard you. Grace will cover you. And God will honor you for choosing integrity over image, truth over terror, and holiness over hypocrisy.

CHAPTER 19

Keys to Choosing a Good Mate, Wisdom Before the Wedding

In a world filled with romantic myths, hasty decisions, and emotional entanglements, choosing the right life partner is one of the most significant and spiritual decisions a person will ever make. Marriage is not merely a social contract—it is a covenant, a joining of destinies, purposes, and legacies. While love is essential, love alone is not enough. Wisdom, discernment, character, and spiritual alignment must guide the process. The difference between peace and pain, growth and grief, or destiny and disaster often lies in the choice of a mate.

This chapter explores the keys to choosing a good mate—laying out biblical principles, emotional intelligence, character discernment, and practical wisdom. It also presents a critical section on non-negotiables and a sobering examination of red flags that cannot be ignored.

I. Choosing with Vision, Not Just Emotion

The emotions of attraction can be strong, even overwhelming. Chemistry may spark, conversations may flow, and compatibility may seem instant. But wise mate selection requires seeing beyond feelings and into the future. **Proverbs 19:2** warns, *"Desire without knowledge is not good—how much more will hasty feet miss the way!"*

When choosing a mate, ask yourself: Can this person build with me? Do they respect my values, purpose, and calling? Do they have a sense of vision beyond today? **Amos 3:3** asks, *"Can two walk together unless they are agreed?"* That agreement must go deeper than hobbies or surface preferences—it must touch on faith, finances, family goals, and moral convictions.

A good mate doesn't just make you feel good—they make you grow. They won't just compliment your beauty—they will strengthen your integrity. They won't only stimulate your desires—they'll sharpen your destiny.

II. Character Over Charisma

Many have been deceived by charm, only to find themselves married to someone who performs well in public but behaves like a tyrant in private. Charm is not character. A good mate must be assessed not by how they present themselves on dates, but by how they handle disappointment, delay, and disagreement.

Proverbs 31:30 declares, *"Charm is deceitful, and beauty is vain, but a woman who fears the Lord is to be praised."* The same principle applies to men. A handsome face and eloquent tongue mean little if the man lacks integrity, humility, and consistency.

Character shows up in the little things:

- How do they treat service workers?
- Do they apologize sincerely when wrong?
- Are they accountable to anyone?
- Do they lie, justify bad behavior, or shift blame?

Jesus said in **Matthew 7:16**, *"By their fruit you will recognize them."* Not their potential, not their words—their fruit. A good mate produces fruit worthy of love, honor, and covenant.

III. Shared Spiritual Foundation

Marriage was designed by God, and to function as He intended, it must be built on shared spiritual values. **2 Corinthians 6:14** instructs, *"Do not be unequally yoked with unbelievers."* This is not about judgment—it's about alignment. If your spouse does not submit to God, how can they fully honor you? If they do not seek divine guidance, whose voice are they following?

A shared faith:

- Unites you in prayer and worship
- Provides a common moral compass
- Enables you to raise children with unified spiritual values
- Sustains your relationship through storms

Do not compromise on spiritual alignment. Infatuation fades. Beauty ages. But a shared foundation in Christ anchors your relationship in truth and grace.

IV. Emotional Maturity and Communication

Love thrives in emotional safety. A good mate must be able to manage their emotions, communicate clearly, and handle conflict without aggression or withdrawal. As **Proverbs** 16:32 says, *"Better a patient person than a warrior, one with self-control than one who takes a city."*

Ask yourself:

- Can they express feelings without blame?
- Do they resolve disagreements or escalate them?
- Are they defensive or open to correction?
- Do they shut down or engage honestly?

Marriage requires mature communication. A good mate will not ghost, gaslight, or guilt-trip you. They will speak truth in love and invite you into healing conversations, not hostile arguments.

V. The Power of Purpose Compatibility

Purpose is the compass of a relationship. If two people are headed in opposite directions, love will not hold them together. Ask: Does this person's life calling complement mine, or conflict with it?

God joins people for more than romance—He joins them for kingdom assignment. **Genesis 2:18** reveals God's design: *"It is not good for the man to be alone. I will make a helper suitable for him."* The Hebrew word for "helper" is *ezer*—a strong partner, not a servant. A good mate strengthens your purpose.

Consider these questions:

- Are they lazy while you're ambitious?
- Are you mission-driven while they chase pleasure?
- Are they threatened by your dreams or supportive?

These are not small issues—they determine the trajectory of your shared life.

VI. Non-Negotiables — Standards That Must Never Be Compromised

These are traits that must be firmly in place before marriage, regardless of charm or desire. Non-negotiables are not about being picky—they are about protecting your peace, purpose, and future.

1. Faith in Christ

A genuine relationship with Christ is not optional—it is the cornerstone of a healthy Christian marriage. The Bible warns clearly in **2 Corinthians 6:14**, *"Do not be unequally yoked with unbelievers."* This principle protects you from partnering with someone whose values, convictions, and spiritual direction are fundamentally incompatible with yours. A person's relationship with God shapes how they love, forgive, endure trials, and grow. Without that foundation, the covenant of marriage becomes a constant tug-of-war between flesh and faith.

It's not enough for someone to claim they are a Christian. The question is: Do they follow Christ? Do they bear the fruit of the Spirit—love, joy, peace, patience, kindness, goodness, faithfulness, gentleness, and self-control (Galatians 5:22–23)? Do they attend church regularly? Are they submitted to spiritual leadership? Do they spend time in the Word and prayer? A spiritually immature or spiritually indifferent mate will eventually clash with your pursuit of God and may even try to derail it.

Faith in Christ doesn't mean perfection—it means direction. Is your potential mate moving toward God? Are they growing in grace? Are they convicted when they sin? A spouse who honors Christ will be much more likely to honor you. If you marry someone who does not fear God, you may have to fight spiritual battles alone that were meant to be fought together. A shared walk with God is not a bonus—it is a boundary line of wisdom.

2. Emotional Wholeness

Everyone carries scars, but not everyone is emotionally ready for marriage. Emotional wounds that are not healed often manifest in destructive patterns like manipulation, defensiveness, passive aggression, or withdrawal. **Proverbs 4:23** reminds us, *"Above all else, guard your heart, for everything you do flows from it."* An emotionally unhealthy person will bring toxicity into the relationship, even if they mean well. Love alone cannot fix brokenness that the individual refuses to address.

Pay attention to how they talk about their past—do they take ownership or blame everyone else? Are they still bitter about a former relationship? Do they explode under pressure or shut down during conflict? Emotional immaturity shows up in how people handle criticism, disappointment, and change. Marriage will expose every unresolved trauma. If they haven't done the inner work of healing, you may become the casualty of their unresolved issues.

Seek someone who is self-aware, emotionally intelligent, and committed to growth. Do they know their triggers? Are they willing to seek counseling when necessary? Can they manage their moods without lashing out? The ability to apologize, listen, and regulate emotions is not just nice—it's necessary. A whole heart loves well. A broken heart, left unchecked, wounds others.

3. Financial Responsibility

Marriage is not just a union of hearts—it's a merger of households, and finances play a major role in marital peace. **Proverbs 13:11** says, *"Dishonest money dwindles away, but whoever gathers money little by little makes it grow."* A potential mate's financial habits reveal a great deal about their discipline, foresight, and sense of responsibility. It is not wealth that makes someone suitable for marriage—it is their stewardship.

If someone is drowning in debt, lives beyond their means, or has no budget, these are not minor issues—they are red flags. Financial irresponsibility can lead to chronic stress, conflict, and even poverty. Ask yourself: Do they pay their bills on time? Do they save, tithe, and give? Are they willing to live within their means? Do they have a job and a vision for financial growth? Marrying someone with no money plan is like boarding a ship with no captain.

Money habits are often tied to values. Does your potential spouse honor God with their finances? Do they treat money as a tool or as a god? Are they generous or greedy? These habits will not magically change after marriage. A partner with sound financial responsibility will not only provide stability but will build a **legacy** with you. Choose someone with vision, not just spending power.

4. Respect for Boundaries

Healthy boundaries are the invisible fences that protect identity, respect, and freedom in a relationship. When someone ignores or repeatedly violates your boundaries, it's not just inconsiderate—it's dangerous. Proverbs 25:17 says, "Let your foot rarely be in your neighbor's house, or he will become weary of you and hate you." Even Scripture teaches that overstepping boundaries leads to resentment.

Watch how your potential mate responds when you say "no." Do they get angry, sulk, guilt-trip you, or respect your decision? Do they press for more physical intimacy than you're comfortable with? Do they manipulate spiritual concepts like submission to control you? A person who won't respect your emotional, physical, or spiritual limits while dating will almost certainly trample them after marriage.

Respect for boundaries also includes time, space, and family relationships. Do they demand all your time? Are they jealous of your friends, work, or ministry commitments? Do they give you room to grow independently? A healthy relationship is one where freedom and accountability coexist. Someone who respects your boundaries respects you.

5. Accountability to Others

No one is above correction. Even Jesus, though sinless, lived in submission to the Father and obeyed His will. Hebrews 13:17 says, "Obey your leaders and submit to them, for they keep watch over your souls." A person who refuses to be accountable to mentors, leaders, or spiritual authorities is a danger to themselves and others.

Ask: Who do they answer to? Who can correct them? Who do they turn to for wisdom? If they isolate themselves or claim they "only listen to God," be careful—that often means they are unteachable and proud. Accountability is the safeguard of humility. It creates space for counsel, correction, and community. Without it, your future spouse can become an uncontrollable force that wrecks your peace.

Also pay attention to how they treat mentors. Do they speak well of their pastors or mentors? Do they receive counsel with gratitude or resentment? Do they make major decisions without guidance? Accountability is not control—it is covering. When storms come (and they will), a spouse with godly accountability won't rely on ego—they will lean into wisdom. That makes all the difference.

6. Shared Life Vision

Love without shared direction is like two people on a train heading in opposite directions—it may feel good now, but separation is inevitable. Amos 3:3 asks, "Can two walk together unless they have agreed to do so?" Life vision involves calling, career goals, family structure, ministry, lifestyle, and priorities. Compatibility in these areas ensures long-term unity.

Do they want children? Do you? Do they want to live overseas while you want to plant roots? Do they support your calling or resent it? Do they value church involvement or see it as optional? These are not secondary questions—they are foundational. Purpose must be aligned for peace to be preserved. You may fall in love with someone's heart but suffer from their direction.

It's not just about shared goals—it's about shared timing and pace. One may want to marry immediately; the other may want to wait five years. One may want to build a business; the other prefers a secure paycheck. Neither is wrong—but you must agree. A shared vision means you build toward the same future, not pull each other in opposite directions.

7. Integrity

At the core of a trustworthy relationship is truth. Proverbs 10:9 says, "Whoever walks in integrity walks securely, but he who makes his ways crooked will be found out." Integrity is doing what's right even when no one is watching. It's telling the truth, keeping promises, and living consistently in private and public. Without it, your marriage will be built on sand.

People without integrity lie, exaggerate, cover their flaws, and manipulate reality to protect themselves. They may cheat in small ways, dismiss truth as "harmless," and make excuses for betrayal. A person who casually breaks small promises will likely break larger covenants. Trust is not something you gamble with—it is something you guard.

Integrity is proven over time. It is seen in how they speak about others, how they handle money, how they honor their commitments, and how they treat those who cannot benefit them. A person of integrity builds a relationship you can rest in. When storms come—and they will—their integrity becomes your peace. Do not marry someone you cannot believe.

VII. Red Flags — Signals You Must Not Ignore

These signs indicate potential for abuse, dysfunction, or long-term misery if overlooked.

1. Lack of Accountability

A man who answers to no one is a danger to everyone. Refusing accountability reveals pride, rebellion, and the potential for secret sin. **Proverbs 12:15** declares, *"The way of a fool is right in his own eyes, but a wise man listens to advice."* If he cannot be corrected by others, you will not be able to correct him either. Marriage requires mutual submission, and a man unwilling to submit is unfit to lead.

Look at the spiritual structure of his life. Is he mentored by godly men? Does he take advice from pastors, counselors, or older, wiser individuals? If not, who holds him to godly standards? Unaccountable men are often masters at hiding sin, manipulating people, and shifting blame. Accountability is not a sign of weakness—it is a shield against deception. When a man has no one who can speak into his life, he becomes a law unto himself.

An unaccountable man will often shut down conversations, become defensive when confronted, or spiritualize rebellion by claiming, "Only God can judge me." These are red flags of a hidden agenda. Submission to godly authority does not make a man less masculine—it proves his maturity. If he is evasive about his relationships with mentors or unwilling to invite spiritual oversight, it's a sign that he is unsafe. Never marry a man who answers to no one.

2. Disrespect for Women

How a man treats women—especially those who cannot benefit him—is a litmus test of his heart. If he demeans, mocks, or belittles women in conversation or behavior, believe him the first time. **1 Peter 3:7** says, *"Husbands, live with your wives in an understanding way, showing honor... so that your prayers may not be hindered."* Disrespect toward women is not a quirk—it's a curse.

Watch how he treats waitresses, cashiers, or female relatives. Does he interrupt, talk over, or dismiss women's opinions? Does he refer to women in degrading terms, even in jokes? These are not harmless flaws—they are indicators of deeply rooted misogyny. A man who scorns women will eventually mistreat his wife—emotionally, mentally, or even physically. Marriage will not change that; it will amplify it.

Many women ignore this red flag because they feel "special" or "different," believing they will be treated better. But the truth is, the pattern will continue. If he disrespects his mother, dishonors his ex, or looks down on female leaders, it's only a matter of time before that disdain turns toward you. A man who honors women reflects Christ, who protected and elevated women. Do not marry a man who mocks what God made sacred.

3. Quick Temper and Uncontrolled Anger

A man with no control over his temper is a walking explosion. **Proverbs 22:24–25** warns, *"Do not make friends with a hot-tempered* *person… or you may learn their ways and get yourself ensnared."* A quick temper may be dismissed as passion or stress, but it is dangerous and destructive—especially in marriage. Unchecked anger leads to verbal abuse, emotional damage, and even physical violence.

Pay attention to how he responds when things don't go his way. Does he yell, throw things, curse, or slam doors? Does he blame others for his outbursts or claim, "That's just how I am"? These are not personality traits—they are threats to your peace and safety. Even if he has not directed anger at you yet, it is only a matter of time. People often show their worst sides when they feel secure. Marriage offers that security.

An angry man is also emotionally unpredictable. One moment he is charming, the next he is raging. This creates an environment of fear and instability, especially for children. James 1:20 reminds us, "Human anger does not produce the righteousness that God desires." A godly man must be slow to anger, not quick to wrath. Rage is not romance. Passion is not fury. Do not confuse volatility with strength. It is a red flag that should never be ignored.

4. Addictions

Addictions—whether to substances, pornography, gambling, or even social media—are clear signs of bondage. **2 Peter 2:19** says, *"A man is a slave to whatever has mastered him."* Addiction is not just a personal issue—it becomes a marital crisis. Addicts often lie, steal, and manipulate to protect their habit. The addiction becomes the third party in the marriage, constantly demanding attention, money, and secrecy.

Addiction reveals deep emotional wounds and a lack of coping skills. Until those are addressed and healed, marriage only complicates the struggle. Many women believe they can "love him into healing," but that's a dangerous illusion. Addiction must be confronted through accountability, counseling, and deliverance—not through romance. If he is not actively pursuing sobriety and healing before marriage, he likely never will.

Even in recovery, the signs of true transformation must be evident: humility, consistency, transparency, and support systems. Beware of secretive behavior, sudden disappearances, or mood swings. If he hides his phone, avoids questions, or shows signs of withdrawal from normal life, take heed. Addiction is a thief—it steals joy, trust, intimacy, and future stability. Don't marry someone who is married to their vice.

5. Lies and Half-Truths

Truth is the foundation of trust, and without trust, there can be no safe marriage. **John 8:44** says the devil is the *"father of lies,"* and anyone who continually lies is aligning themselves with deception. A man who tells small lies will eventually tell bigger ones. Lying is not about protecting feelings—it's about control and concealment.

If he frequently changes his story, avoids direct questions, or gets defensive when you seek clarity, beware. These are signs of manipulation. He may hide things under the guise of privacy, but privacy is different from secrecy. A trustworthy man brings his whole self to the relationship. Transparency is not optional—it's foundational.

Watch for inconsistencies in his words and actions. Does he say he's saved but lives sinfully? Does he claim to love you but hide you from his life? Does he dodge accountability or ghost you during conflict? These are not romantic mysteries—they are escape routes. A man who cannot walk in truth will create a home full of confusion, suspicion, and emotional damage. Love demands honesty. Lies are love's poison.

6. Controlling Behavior

Control is often mistaken for leadership, but it is rooted in fear, insecurity, and ego. Galatians 5:1 reminds us, "It is for freedom that

Christ has set us free." A controlling man will dictate how you dress, who you talk to, what you do, and where you go—not out of love, but out of a need to dominate. He wants power, not partnership.

Pay attention to how he reacts when you disagree. Does he guilt-trip, isolate, or punish you emotionally? Does he require constant access to your phone or social media? Does he speak for you in public or interrupt your opinions? These are signs that he does not see you as an equal, but as property. Control is not protection—it is a cage. And the longer you stay, the smaller your voice becomes.

Some controlling men even use Scripture as a weapon, twisting verses like "wives submit to your husbands" to enforce blind obedience. But biblical leadership is rooted in love, not tyranny. Christ leads the church with grace, sacrifice, and service—not domination. If you feel suffocated, fearful, or small around him, don't call it love. Call it what it is: abuse in disguise.

7. Spiritual Immaturity

Spiritual immaturity in a man means you will have to carry the spiritual weight of the marriage alone. Hebrews 5:12–14 rebukes those who, by now, should be teachers but still need spiritual milk. A man who lacks hunger for God, avoids church, or mocks spiritual discipline is not prepared to lead a godly home. You cannot build a spiritual life on a flesh-driven foundation.

Watch his spiritual habits. Does he pray regularly, study the Word, fast, and submit to godly leadership? Or is his spiritual life a performance—only activated when convenient or when you're watching? Spiritual immaturity shows up in a lack of conviction, compromise, and confusion. If he can't lead himself in the Word, he cannot lead you.

Don't settle for a man who is physically attractive but spiritually passive. His title—Christian—means nothing without fruit. The man who will lead your household must first know how to kneel before

God. Don't marry potential. Marry **proof**. Spiritual maturity is not about knowing all the answers—it's about walking with God daily. A man without it will not cover you; he will cost you.

VIII. God's Peace as the Ultimate Guide

Colossians 3:15 says, "Let the peace of Christ rule in your hearts." The Greek word for "rule" here is the same as "umpire"—a judge who determines what stays and what goes. Peace is not just a feeling; it's a **confirmation**. If God's peace lifts when you're around someone, don't ignore it.

Fast. Pray. Wait. Watch. Ask mentors. Evaluate the fruit. Let the Holy Spirit confirm what your emotions cannot. If God says "no," it's because His "yes" is better.

Choose With Eyes Wide Open

Choosing a good mate is not luck—it's wisdom. It requires prayer, observation, discernment, and community. Don't choose out of desperation, loneliness, or sexual desire. Don't ignore red flags and call it grace. And don't compromise non-negotiables and call it love.

Marriage is more than a ceremony—it is a journey of purpose, partnership, and sometimes pain. Who you choose determines how well you walk. So choose wisely. Choose prayerfully. And most of all, choose with **God at the center.**

The right mate will not complete you—but they will **complement** you. They will not manipulate your calling—but magnify it. They will not bring confusion—but clarity. And when you find them, you'll realize—they were worth the wait.

Conclusion

From Miserable to Mighty — The Exit from Bondage

If you've made it to the final page of this book, something in you already knows: this isn't just a collection of case studies—it's a mirror of pain, a manual of truth, and a mantle of permission. Permission to feel, to name, to heal, and, if necessary, to leave what God never intended for you to endure.

The purpose of *Dangerous Dudes* was never to villainize men—it was to vindicate the woman who has spent years second-guessing her own sanity. It was to name the patterns that wear religious clothing but speak the language of control, deception, passivity, entitlement, and emotional starvation. Whether you are dealing with a Narcissist who makes everything about himself, a Dream Killer who suffocates your potential, or a Religious Manipulator who distorts Scripture to dominate your spirit, this book was written to expose the dysfunction and liberate your soul.

The truth is, many women are more married to the fantasy of who a man could become than the reality of who he is. They stay, hoping he'll change. They pray, fast, and bend themselves into pretzels, trying to be "better" so he'll love them right. But healing doesn't happen in the shadows. It begins with truth. Jesus said, *"You shall know the truth, and the truth shall make you free"* **(John 8:32)**. Truth is your doorway out. But courage is the step you must take through it.

If you've recognized your story in these pages, let me be clear: you are not crazy, bitter, or rebellious. You are a woman made in the image of God who deserves to be treated with dignity, tenderness, and respect. You are not required to die on the altar of loyalty to a man who has buried you beneath his dysfunction. God loves you too much to let you stay bound. He came to set captives free—even if that captivity wears a wedding band.

To every woman who is still holding on: ask yourself, *Is this making me holy—or just miserable?* God does not bless abuse. He does not endorse control. He does not partner with manipulation. And He never called you to stay in something that is slowly dismantling the woman He created you to be.

To the men who've read this far with humility—there is still time to change. Repentance is not shame—it is transformation. It is the bridge from brokenness to wholeness. Don't defend your dysfunction. Don't hide behind Scripture to justify sin. Be the kind of man your wife can trust, honor, and thrive with.

To the church, counselors, and leaders: we must do better. We must stop telling women to pray their way through hell while holding men to no account. We must stop using verses about submission while ignoring verses about love, sacrifice, and servant-leadership. Silence in the face of abuse is complicity. Neutrality is protection for the predator—not the victim.

And finally, to every woman reading this with tears in her eyes and hope barely flickering in her heart—this is not the end of your story. There is life after him. There is peace on the other side of pain. And there is a God who still fights for the broken, binds up the wounded, and specializes in raising women from the ashes of betrayal into beauty and boldness.

DEADLY DUDES

You were never created to be miserable. You were made to be mighty. So rise. Walk out of the confusion. Step into clarity. And never again mistake endurance for godliness when God has called you to freedom. This is your exodus. This is your healing. This is your time.

With fierce hope,

APPENDICES

Appendix A

10 Powerful Scriptures for Discernment and Wisdom in Relationships

1. **Proverbs 4:23** — *"Above all else, guard your heart, for everything you do flows from it."*
   → Your heart is not a toy or testing ground. Guard it from manipulative charm and counterfeit love.
2. **James 1:5** — *"If any of you lacks wisdom, let him ask of God... and it will be given to him."*
   → Wisdom is the key to choosing the right mate. You're not alone—ask God, and He will answer.
3. **Proverbs 22:24-25** — *"Do not make friends with a hot-tempered person... or you may learn their ways and get yourself ensnared."*
   → Toxic traits are contagious. Be watchful of who you emotionally attach to.
4. **2 Timothy 3:1-5** — A list of red flags: lovers of self, abusive, unloving, unforgiving, lovers of pleasure rather than God.
   → Don't ignore these signs. The Bible already warned us what the last days would look like in relationships.
5. **Matthew 7:16** — *"You will know them by their fruits."*
   → Don't be deceived by words—watch the pattern of their behavior.
6. **1 Corinthians 13:4–7** — *"Love is patient, love is kind... it does not dishonor others."*

→ This is God's definition of love. Anything less is not love.

7. **Proverbs 31:11–12** — *"The heart of her husband trusts in her... She brings him good, not harm."*

   → A healthy relationship is marked by mutual trust and blessing, not harm and fear.

8. **Colossians 3:19** — *"Husbands, love your wives and do not be harsh with them."*

   → Harshness is not a personality trait—it's disobedience to God's Word.

9. **Ephesians 5:25** — "Husbands, love your wives as Christ loved the Church and gave Himself for her."

   → Sacrificial love is the model, not selfish dominance.

10. **1 Peter 3:7** — *"Husbands, dwell with your wives with understanding... so your prayers may not be hindered."*

    → Mistreating a wife has spiritual consequences—even your prayers are affected.

Appendix B

10 Affirmations for Women in Toxic Relationships

1. I am not crazy—I am discerning what's unhealthy and unholy.
2. God does not require me to stay in bondage to prove my loyalty.
3. I am worthy of love, respect, honesty, and safety.
4. I can leave without guilt when staying means losing myself.
5. My voice matters, even if it's been silenced before.
6. God cares more about my healing than about public appearances.
7. My emotions are valid. My instincts are a gift.
8. I refuse to normalize spiritual, emotional, or verbal abuse.
9. I am not called to save a man who won't save himself.
10. I have a future filled with peace, love, and restoration.

Appendix c

Dangerous Dudes Reflection Checklist

Use this checklist to reflect on your relationship or potential partner. If multiple items are consistently "Yes," seek godly counsel and consider emotional safety a priority.

- Does he frequently belittle or mock you in private or public?
- Does he use Scripture to justify his superiority or control?
- Does he make you feel responsible for his moods, failures, or anger?
- Do you feel like you're walking on eggshells around him?
- Is he overly secretive, defensive, or manipulative?
- Does he isolate you from friends, family, or support systems?
- Does he minimize or dismiss your feelings and concerns?
- Does he refuse accountability or become hostile when corrected?
- Is your spiritual life stifled because of his control or hypocrisy?
- Are you more afraid than fulfilled in this relationship?

Appendix D

Safe Exit Planning for Women in Harmful Relationships

Note: If you are in danger or experiencing abuse, contact a professional or domestic violence hotline immediately.

- Create a secret emergency bag (ID, keys, bank info, medicine).
- Inform a trusted friend or counselor about your situation.
- Secure copies of important documents and financial accounts.
- Keep a private journal of toxic or abusive incidents for accountability.
- Set emotional boundaries and spiritual clarity through prayer and support.
- Know that leaving for safety is not rebellion—it's wisdom.

Appendix E

Recommended Books and Resources

Books
- Why Does He Do That? by Lundy Bancroft
- The Emotionally Destructive Marriage by Leslie Vernick
- *Boundaries in Marriage* by Dr. Henry Cloud & Dr. John Townsend
- *Love Must Be Tough* by Dr. James Dobson
- Is It Me? Making Sense of Your Confusing Marriage by Natalie Hoffman

Websites and Ministries
- Focus on the Family (www.focusonthefamily.com)
- The Hotline – Domestic Abuse Resources (www.thehotline.org)
- Flying Free Sisterhood (www.flyingfreenow.com)
- Leslie Vernick (www.leslievernick.com)
- AACC Christian Counselors Directory (www.aacc.net)

Appendix F

Prayers for Discernment, Strength, and Healing

Prayer for Discernment:

"Lord, open my eyes to see clearly. Remove confusion and fear. If this relationship is not from You, give me the boldness to let go and the wisdom to walk away. Speak to me through Your Spirit, confirm through Your Word, and send wise counsel to guide my steps. Amen."

Prayer for Strength:

"Father, I feel weak, weary, and afraid. But I know You are my strength. Help me to rise above manipulation, shame, and control. Restore my courage, restore my peace, and restore my voice. I refuse to be silent in the face of sin. I receive boldness in Jesus' name."

Prayer for Healing:

"Jesus, You are the Healer of the brokenhearted. Touch every place in me that's been bruised by betrayal, dishonor, or fear. Restore my soul. Heal my memories. Remove every lie that was spoken over me. Make me whole again, and teach me how to trust Your love."

DEADLY DUDES

www.ingramcontent.com/pod-product-compliance
Lightning Source LLC
Chambersburg PA
CBHW071118160426
43196CB00013B/2618